Exploring Options

A Practical Guide to Options Trading

C. DOUGLAS FOX

THE GLOBE AND MAIL

Penguin Books

PENGUIN BOOKS
Published by the Penguin Group
Penguin Books Canada Ltd., 10 Alcorn Avenue, Suite 300, Toronto, Canada M4V 3B2
Penguin Books Limited, 27 Wrights Lane, London W8 5TZ, England
Viking Penguin Inc., 40 West 23rd Street, New York, New York 10010, U.S.
Penguin Books Australia Ltd., Ringwood, Victoria, Australia
Penguin Books (NZ) Ltd., 182-190 Wairau Road, Auckland 10, New Zealand
Penguin Books Ltd., Registered Offices: Harmondsworth, Middlesex, England
Published in Penguin Books, 1996

10 9 8 7 6 5 4 3 2 1

Copyright © Globe Information Services, 1996

All enquiries should be addressed to Globe Information Services, 444 Front Street West,
Toronto, Ontario M5V 2S9, (416) 585-5250

Canadian Cataloguing in Publication Data
The National Library of Canada has catalogued this publication as follows:
Fox, C. Douglas
    Exploring options: a practical guide to options trading

(Globe and Mail personal finance library)
1996-
Annual.

ISSN 1204-3680
ISBN 0-14-025620-2 (1996 issue)

1. Derivative securities – Periodicals.   2. Options (Finance) – Periodicals.
3. Stock options – Periodicals.   I. Series

HG6024.C3E96   332.64'5'05   C96-900129-0

Cover design: Creative Network
Cover illustration: Peter Yundt
Charts: Ivy Wong

CONTENTS

PART V
PUTTING IT TOGETHER

Tables and Illustrations

Dedication

This book is dedicated to my mother who kept me company through weeks of typing at Raven Lake.

Acknowledgments

ONE HAS ONLY TO WRITE A BOOK TO discover the help and support needed to complete the task. Writing is a somewhat solitary experience and one is continually in need of input and encouragement from others. At the outset, it begins with prompting from friends to attempt the task. The process continues with the support of colleagues and expert advice. When you get close to completion, you suddenly realize the many contributions made by others, from simple encouragement to technical advice, that made the project possible. A special acknowledgment is due to my research assistant Mary Kwok for her contributions to Chapters 1, 2, 14 and 15; and for her many hours of painstaking research — thanks. And to Paul Bates, Chris Climo, Roy Dalton, Alan Husdal, David Lapansee, Elaine Wyatt, June Yee and Susan Yee, my sincerest thanks.

c.d.f.

Introduction

THE FIRST VISIT TO A MAJOR
stock or option exchange is invariably a memorable experience for
any investor. As you approach the trading floor, the din grows and
grows. Eventually your escort is screaming in your ear attempting to
explain the commotion while people in multicoloured jackets rush
past you frantically writing, shouting or waving to some counterpart
amid the throng of thousands. The Chicago Board Options Exchange has signs that say "No Standing." Indeed, motion is almost
self-defence for the uninitiated. The many computer terminals and
the activity of the traders provide heat year-round for the entire
trading floor, as well as the floor above it. The noise level is so high
that a loud speaking voice is virtually a prerequisite for employ-
ment. When I worked on the Toronto Stock Exchange as a trader,
my boss told me to practice shouting in front of a mirror to improve
my communication skills.

The glamour of the options market only begins with the excitement of the trading floor. Whether an expert or novice investor, options offer more scope for investing than any other single
investment vehicle. This book is not only about options, it is about
using options for investment rather than speculation. Let's be realis-
tic: To be a speculator all you need to do is put your money down,
pick up the dice and let them fly. Granted, the options market provides a wonderful place to do this in — it can even provide you
with more bang for your buck. But the average investor, like you
and me, works hard for his money and seeks secure, steady gains
while preserving his capital. The options industry has grown to realize this. In the many conferences I attend each year, the typical
themes are enhancing portfolio performance, hedging assets, diversification and transferring risk. Who are the largest option traders in
today's market? Pension fund managers, mutual fund managers,

portfolio managers and banks. Do these sound like speculators to you?

With all the negative press surrounding listed options, you might wonder why people trade them at all. Anyone who has ever heard of options has heard that they are risky. Let me only say that if you speculate, you are taking risks. You may speculate with many types of securities. If, for instance, you invest everything you have in one stock, and perhaps margin that stock as well, then you are taking a very great risk. It doesn't matter which stock you decide to purchase, whether the best of the blue chips or the smallest of the penny stocks. Depending solely on one security puts you at great risk. Your loss will be profound if that one stock declines.

After a review of option basics, I will analyze many option strategies. Some of the more advanced strategies may benefit you solely on an intellectual level, but they will give you a feeling for the flexibility of options and how professionals use them. My focus will be on the more practical strategies. Even the choice between buying a call option or buying the underlying stock can be critical. My intent is to arm you with strategies that will help you deal with various circumstances. I will also encourage you to select only a few strategies and to stick with the ones that you are most comfortable with.

I have included a special section dealing with the relatively long dated options known as LEAPS, a registered trademark of the Chicago Board Options Exchange. I believe LEAPS are the most exciting new option product to come to the marketplace in many years. I will also spend some time describing other listed derivatives which have been gaining popularity in recent years. The most viable of these are the so-called basket securities. Futures and some of the more arcane derivatives that trade over-the-counter will also be discussed.

Finally, I assume that you are a lot like me when it comes to investing: A below-average stock picker with moderate capital. I have written this book to demystify the options market for the beginner, enhance the knowledge of the average investor and, in general, improve your results in the market.

CHAPTER 1

Why Use Options?

OPTIONS HAVE BEEN USED throughout history and from ancient times to today. They have not always been called options but the same basic characteristics have been present in these primitive investment tools as in the listed options contracts which trade on exchanges today. They have always granted the holder the right to exercise and take or sell an underlying interest; and the seller has always been obligated to deliver or take delivery of the same underlying interest. Prior to becoming regulated in the 20th century, however, they typically came in to play whenever there was some speculative uprising in financial or commodity markets.

Lessons from history

In the early 17th century, Holland witnessed one of the most frenzied incidents of speculation in financial history. The tulip bulb craze, or "tulipmania," began with an appreciation for a rare Mediterranean member of the lily family. The desire to own tulip bulbs grew and grew until it reached a frenzied height. By 1630, investment in tulip bulbs had gripped the entire country, and some neighbouring countries as well.

People would buy and sell tulips for vast sums, $50,000 in today's money, even while they were still unseen in the ground. This speculation eventually spawned a market in future tulips. Growers would buy contracts which guaranteed the price of future crops, put options, and speculators would purchase contracts granting them the right to buy them, call options, in the hope that they would be worth more than their present-day value. This incredible story eventually ended as all speculative stories do, with everyone losing their money. The price of a tulip eventually dropped to its proper value and buyers of these futures contracts refused to honour their obligations to purchase them at the agreed-upon price. Today, we have established clearing-houses which guarantee the value of options and futures contracts. The owner of a modern-day future or option is assured that whatever the financial health of the person he purchased his contract from, he will still be able to collect his profit.

The South Sea Bubble is a name given to a speculative boom which occurred in England in the 18th century. Again, a frenzied demand grew for shares in a South Sea trading company. In this case it led to highly leveraged purchases on margin and future promises to purchase at predetermined prices. Eventually, the bubble burst when it was discovered that there was no underlying value to these shares. When it was discovered that company insiders were dumping their shares on the market, the price quickly plummeted.

Amazingly enough, options were actually blamed for the crash in price of these shares and trading in them was outlawed until the 19th century. Sound familiar? Of course, just as mistakenly, history repeated itself after the October, 1987, stock market crash with options and program trading being unjustly blamed for the financial ruin of equity markets. Even today, options are constantly in the press as the evil in today's financial markets. No mention is ever given to massive or unwarranted speculation, or even the misuse of these instruments. Knowledge of these events from history should be required reading for anyone entering into the world of investing. And if you are tempted to say that it could never happen today, just consider the real estate losses across North America in the late 1980s, especially in Ontario. How many times have we heard it repeated that real estate was the "best investment" and that you couldn't lose money in real estate. I suppose that the reason options are so often blamed is that investors lack an understanding of them. If certain investors were to lose a large sum trading penny stocks, it is unlikely that the government would step in and outlaw penny stocks. The moral of the story is that you will usually find speculation at the forefront of any financial collapse; and it is not the trading instruments which caused the actual losses but the manner in which they were used.

In the 20th century, options began to trade over the counter. Broker-dealers in the United States would quote prices on puts and calls in the financial press. Eventually it became clear that this new trading instrument required an organized exchange of its own, and in 1973, the Chicago Board Options Exchange (CBOE) opened its doors. Many other existing exchanges began to trade options in 1975: the Toronto Stock Exchange, the Sydney Stock Exchange, the American Stock Exchange and the Philadelphia Stock Exchange. The importance of this was that options started to be regulated and standardized. Traders could readily buy and sell a standard contract that was properly defined by a stock exchange and guaranteed by a clearing-house.

Eventually options became available on several different underlying interests: bonds, currencies and even indices. From an initial volume of only 911 contracts on the opening day of the CBOE in 1973, trading has grown to over 2,000 contracts per minute in the United States alone.

An investment tool

Options are often called an investment tool. They are something that should be used in conjunction with several other tools. You normally would not build a house using only one tool. Nor should you build a portfolio using a single investment strategy. In my personal portfolio, I have some government coupons, the occasional T-bill, some money market funds, some long stock, some short stock and some short put options. This is what I consider an average portfolio in terms of risk. With the exception of the long and short stock there is very little risk. The short put options are a quiet strategy designed to make a small profit over a certain period of time. The security underlying the put options is the stock of a Canadian Schedule A bank. Note that it is the weighting, and not the type, of each component of the portfolio that defines the total risk. In my case, the government coupons represent 80 per cent of the account. This makes it a conservative account with the objective of long-term appreciation and preservation of capital. If I changed the weighting of the coupons to 20 per cent, my account would then be aggressive. Whatever your objectives, options can have a place in your portfolio.

You should decide what your objectives are and ensure that they meet your financial needs. More importantly, you should have the discipline to stick to your objectives. In fact, securities regulations require that your broker ask you for these objectives before executing any trades for you. In choosing your objectives, it is helpful to decide how much risk you are willing to accept. Personally, I hate losing money and I'm not exactly the world's greatest stock picker. I like to keep my risk level low. This approach is in keeping with the advice of most investment advisers. Most advisers tell you to set aside a maximum of 10 to 15 per cent of your portfolio as risk capital. The biggest mistake small investors continue to make is to use too big a portion of their capital for a single trade.

You cannot make decisions that are based on emotion and fear when trading in the stock market. And rest assured, emotions will cloud your decision-making when you are faced with a loss of 30 per cent or more for a single trade. You might be tempted to remain in the market when the only sensible action is to exit the trade. This type of thinking will lead to the depletion of your capital. To paraphrase Falstaff, "He who fights and runs away lives to fight another day," serves us well in the options market. For any single options trade, you should plan to use only 10 per cent of the capital you have allotted for short-term gains. This formula will keep you thinking clearly, and keep you in the game. But I will never make any money this way you say. Wrong. When you make a winning trade, the gains can be quite dramatic. But only if your option purchases are made within the framework of proper money management. These gains are made possible through the use of leverage.

Leverage

Simple mathematics will show you that if you double your money when you execute a winning trade, then it is only necessary to make a winning trade four out of every 10 times. Let's say you begin with $1,000 of risk capital. Using our formula, you invest 10 per cent of that capital for a single trade, and repeat the process over the course of 10 trades. If you double your money on four out of 10 trades the outcome will look like Table I.

We have ignored brokerage commissions in this example but rest assured they will eat into your portfolio. I suggest that you amend your capital base slightly to account for commissions by calculating the average amount your broker will charge you for your average-size trade. The formula can be amended to be more conservative or more aggressive depending on your investment objectives.

The above money management strategy is, admittedly, somewhat aggressive. Notice that even though the portfolio value declines to $400 by the end of the sixth trade, the amount of the next trade is still $100. This represents 25 per cent of the remaining portfolio value. You could adjust this formula to maintain an investment of

Using 10 Per Cent of Your Portfolio as Risk Capital

Trade	Amount invested	Gain/Loss	Portfolio value
1	$100	-100%	$ 900
2	$100	-100%	$ 800
3	$100	-100%	$ 700
4	$100	-100%	$ 600
5	$100	-100%	$ 500
6	$100	-100%	$ 400
7	$100	+200%	$ 600
8	$100	+200%	$ 800
9	$100	+200%	$1,000
10	$100	+200%	$1,200

TABLE I

only 10 per cent of the existing portfolio. Thus, beginning with a portfolio of $1,000, after a losing trade of $100, or 10 per cent, the next trade could be adjusted to represent 10 per cent of the remaining $900, or $90. The math would look like Table II.

Note that in each of these investment models we have assumed the worst case: that the losing trades were all done when the portfolio was at its highest value. We have also assumed that in each of the losing trades the entire investment was lost; which need not always be the case. In fact, I will be showing you ways of purchasing calls and puts which will make it extremely rare to lose 100 per cent of your investment. But after six losing trades in a row, the portfolio value is still over half of its original size. This type of investment strategy gives you a tremendous amount of staying power. With proper money management you will be very much "in the game" even after suffering many losing trades in a row.

Further adjustments are possible with this type of money management strategy. You can put aside any profits received once they exceed the $1,000 threshold and never have more than 10 per cent of your original capital invested, a conservative approach. Or simply add the profits to your portfolio for the purposes of calculating the 10 per cent amount of your next trade, an aggressive approach. The point is to maintain a disciplined approach that will limit your losses, allow you to enjoy your gains and let you sleep at night. By "sleeping well at night" I am talking about not allowing emotions to distort your investment decisions.

Using 10 Per Cent of Your Portfolio as Risk Capital, after Adjusting for Commissions

Trade	Amount invested	Gain/Loss	Portfolio value
1	$100	-100%	$ 900
2	$ 90	-100%	$ 810
3	$ 81	-100%	$ 729
4	$ 72	-100%	$ 657
5	$ 65	-100%	$ 592
6	$ 59	-100%	$ 533
7	$ 53	+200%	$ 639
8	$ 64	+200%	$ 767
9	$ 76	+200%	$ 919
10	$ 91	+200%	$1,101

TABLE II

Finally, the above examples assume that the position is always closed out once a profit is reached. There will be times, I hope, that your profit will exceed 200 per cent. In fact, one of the great advantages of options is the ability to enjoy unlimited profits while limiting the risk you assume. The above strategy will not in any way limit the profit potential of your investments. When this happens there are several strategies available to allow you to enjoy continued profits while protecting the ones that you have already realized. These will be discussed in the chapters on option strategies.

The key to these types of strategies is that you must make a trade that has the potential to profit by at least 200 per cent if your forecast is correct. Your forecast must of course be sound if this is going to happen. This is not as daunting a prospect as it first appears.

An example
I recently bought some calls on a Canadian bank stock. They were December 20 calls and cost 75 cents. My reasons were:
- The calls had over three months to expiry and the price of the stock was very near the exercise price of the call, two essential criteria.
- The stock looked good fundamentally, the bank had provided for all their bad loans and the economy was picking up.
- It was perceived that we were in a bull market.

- The dividend yield was higher than the yield on a T-bill and would, I felt, support the share price; there was another dividend due before my calls expired; the stock was trading at $19.87, a new three-year high and a "technical breakout."
- There was good leverage in these particular calls.

Consider this last point: If the shares advanced to $22.25 by the third Saturday in December, I would realize a $1.50 gain — a 200 per cent profit on my original investment. If I were to buy the shares at $19.87 my profit would be $2.37 — an 11.7 per cent return. The leverage of this investment can be seen by the amount of the initial investment required. Paying $75 per call option would afford an exposure to 100 shares of stock, while it would require an investment of $1,987.50 to actually buy 100 shares of the stock. As well, commissions on purchasing options will normally be lower than a corresponding stock purchase. The calls were the better investment.

But the real reason this was a good investment was because of the fundamental reasons described above. Without a good reason to buy the stock there is rarely any reason to buy the options. It goes without saying that the risk of doing this was known: If the shares did not advance beyond $20 by the third week of December, I would lose my entire investment of 75 cents per call. I might also avoid a larger loss by buying the calls instead of the stock if my analysis of the bank proved to be faulty and the share price declined drastically.

To sum up the above example:
- The underlying stock was a good investment for both technical and fundamental reasons.
- There was good leverage in that I could realize the profits from ownership of 1,000 shares of a $20 stock, which would normally require a $20,000 investment, for an investment of $750.
- The profit from the expected or hoped-for move in the underlying shares would produce a 200 per cent return with the call option strategy and only an 11.7 per cent return if the shares were purchased instead.
- The risk of the investment was known and limited to $750.

The only advantage I was giving up to the investor who actually purchased the underlying shares was time. My investment would end by the third Saturday in December, whereas if I had purchased the stock I could continue to hold it and collect a dividend. I would also not be able to receive a dividend like the actual shareholders could. But the amount of the dividend I would receive was also off-set by the cost of the funds necessary to purchase the shares. There are ways to partially offset or minimize the deteriorating effect of time in an option purchase. This will be discussed further in the chapter on LEAPS.

In practice, I tend to use less than 10 per cent of my risk capital but that is due to personal preference. This preference is defined by my ability and desire to assume risk. The point of all this is that with proper money management, a reasonable analysis of the underlying stock and good leverage, you can develop a proper and conservative approach to investing with options.

CHAPTER 2

Terms of the Trade

MAKING AN INVESTMENT should never be a trip into the unknown. Product knowledge is fundamental to understanding the rules of the security you are trading. You are at a serious disadvantage if you are investing in something you do not understand. I remember marvelling one time at the busloads of tourists arriving at a casino in Atlantic City. Most of these people were going to gamble large amounts of money with almost no knowledge of the games they would be playing. They say that an expert blackjack player may get the odds of winning up to approximately 50 per cent. I can't imagine the enormous disadvantage of these beginners, trying to win at a complex game they have never played before. This chapter describes the basic features of options and the way that they are traded. You may wish to skip over some of the concepts covered in this chapter if you are an intermediate to experienced investor, but a review of basics can never do any harm.

Some definitions

Many investors have the impression that options are sophisticated derivative instruments which require complex mathematical calculations in order to be understood. The fact is that option concepts occur in a variety of ways in everyday life. These real-life options are not significantly different from the ones which are listed and trade on stock exchanges. An option is defined as "The right but not the obligation, to acquire, in the case of a call, or to sell, in the case of a put, a specific amount of an agreed-upon security, or underlying interest, at a predetermined price, for a specific period of time."

Any time you are given the right to buy something at a certain price for a given period of time, you possess a call option. This could be a grocery-store coupon offering a discount on the purchase price of a particular product, or a conditional offer you make on the purchase of a house. For instance, let us suppose you offer to purchase an antique car for $20,000, conditional on inspection or financing. No one will give you that option for nothing, of course, so you will have to pay a fee, or premium, for that privilege. The owner will usually charge you a token deposit amount for the right to inspect the car. If for some reason that car appreciates rapidly prior to actually purchasing it, that right to purchase will increase in value accordingly. In other words, by simply purchasing the right to purchase the car you will have already made a profit. This is a simple example of a call option and one of many instances where options exist outside of the stock market.

After purchasing that car, you will probably enter into another type of option transaction by buying automobile insurance. You buy insurance in case the car is stolen or catches on fire and effectively becomes worthless. In this case, you would be able to recover your entire investment, the value of the car minus the cost of the premium paid to insure it. You may plan to sell the car in one year or some other period and, therefore, purchase an insurance contract for that length of time. The insurance is effectively the right to sell at a predetermined price for a certain period of time. This insurance, or put option, effectively locks in the value of your car for a specific period of time.

While by definition an option grants the right but not the obligation to buy or sell, this is only true for the purchaser of the contract — and only for the time defined in the terms of the contract. If the purchaser does not exercise that right within the defined time period, the right will be over; the option will expire. In the above example, the insurance on the car was for a period covering one year. Once the time period of one year passes, the car will no longer be insured.

There are numerous other examples of agreements which are actually option contracts and occur whenever these key concepts are present:

- There is a right to buy and/or sell at a certain price.
- There is a contract covering an agreed-upon quantity.
- The life of the contract is known.

The options market
The above examples of option purchases are only one side of the transaction. Someone must sell this insurance or option in order to

create the contract. The seller, or writer, of that contract must also honour the terms of that agreement if called upon to do so by the buyer, or holder. The writer of the option is therefore obligated to the purchaser but only for the time specified in the contract. In the above example, the insurance company has an obligation equal to the value of the car, for the length of time covered by the insurance policy. Obviously, we would also like some assurance that the insurance company, the writer of the contract, has the financial ability to meet this obligation if called upon to do so.

The option in our example of the antique car is a customized one which is designed solely for the specific needs of an individual investor. The options we will be discussing have standardized features and are known as listed options because they trade on a stock or options exchange, or secondary market. The option in our car example cannot readily be sold because a market does not exist for it. Very few people would have any use for this type of option, so it would be difficult to find a buyer if you wished to liquidate the contract. The only person who may be willing to purchase such a contract if you wished to sell it would be the person who sold the contract to you in the first place. The only way to realize your profit from the car call option is to exercise your option. In other words, buy the car and then sell it to another individual.

However, if an option had standardized features and many people bought and sold options all day long, then it would be a simple matter to sell your option in a secondary market. In the case of listed options, you can avoid the complications of exercising your options by simply selling them on an exchange.

Listed options in North America cover a vast array of financial instruments. Equity options are the most well known, with options on financial indices a close second. Other listed options include Canadian government bonds, gold, silver, currencies, interest rates and futures. There is almost no limit to the number of different instruments an option could cover, though the fact that an option is listed on an exchange does not guarantee that it will be actively traded. Investors may sometimes encounter difficulty attempting to liquidate thinly traded options.

The largest option market in the world is the Chicago Board Options Exchange (CBOE). The most popular option traded there is the Standard & Poor's 100 index option. Its trading symbol is OEX. The trading pit for the OEX option alone is larger than the entire option floor at the Toronto Stock Exchange. In Canada, options trade on all three of the major exchanges: Vancouver, Toronto and Montreal.

In both Canada and the United States, options markets are operated with a market-maker system. Market-makers are individuals who are designated by the particular exchange to run markets in the individual option series. They are normally employed by a firm which is a member of the exchange but can also operate as independent traders. Their job is to ensure there are always bid-ask quotations for each option series. Market-makers are also required to purchase and sell a guaranteed amount of puts or calls at the prices which they post. By guaranteeing that they will purchase or sell a certain number of contracts on the bid or the offer, market-makers provide liquidity in the market.

Standard option features

Imagine the mayhem that would result on an exchange if one investor wanted to purchase an option covering 78 shares and another investor wanted to sell an option for 106 shares. It would be virtually impossible to match the investment needs of buyers and sellers. To simplify things and to make a central trading place possible for options, the specifications for different classes of options have been standardized. There are two types of options: puts and calls. The underlying security on which the option trades is known as a class. The preagreed price denoted by the option is called the exercise price, or strike price. The price of that option trading on an exchange is known as the premium. In North America, each equity option has the following characteristics:

- The contract covers 100 shares of the underlying stock.
- The expiry of the option, its maturity date, is the Saturday following the third Friday of the stated contract month.
- Trading in the option ceases at the same time – usually the close of trading on the exchange – on the Friday preceding the third Saturday of the contract month.
- The option can be exercised at any time during the life of the contract.

To avoid any confusion with actual stocks trading on an exchange I have created a fictitious stock called Popular Gold Stock, and assigned it a trading symbol of PGS. I will be using this stock for virtually all examples in *Exploring Options*. When an option is referred to as a PGS August 40 call, it means that:

- The underlying stock covered by the option is Popular Gold Stock Corporation, 100 shares per contract.
- The option expires in the month of August, on the Saturday following the third Friday.
- The exercise price of the option is $40. When a call is exercised, the holder of the option will purchase the underlying stock at a price of $40.
- The option is a call option; an option is always denoted as a call or a put.

The above call option grants the buyer the right to purchase 100 shares of Popular Gold Stock until the third Saturday in August at $40 per share. An investor who purchases or sells this option is said to be entering an opening transaction. He may subsequently choose to close this position by either buying it back or selling it. Think back to our example of buying the antique car. The buyer purchased the contract but was effectively unable to liquidate or close out the contract because of the absence of a secondary market. When an opening transaction occurs, an initial purchase or sale, the option is actually created by virtue of the agreement between the buyer and seller. The total number of contracts agreed upon between all of the buyers and sellers of any one particular option is known as the open interest.

If this PGS August 40 call is trading in the market at a price of $5.50 then the cost of the option is actually $550. The option covers 100 shares and the premium per share is $5.50. Therefore, the price of the option is 100 multiplied by $5.50, or $550. The price is always multiplied by the total of the underlying shares covered by the option. This factor, the number of shares covered by the option contract, is often referred to as the multiplier.

Option products may differ slightly from exchange to exchange in terms of the time periods, cycles, in which they are listed. The cycle refers to the number of months that a particular class is listed for, usually encompassing at least several months during a nine-month period. The exercise price intervals will also be standardized for any given underlying security or class, and are determined by the price of the underlying shares. There can be several options available on the same stock with the same maturity date and with different strike prices. Options on a stock with a price of $100 will usually have a $5 difference in strike prices, while a $5 stock will normally have intervals as low as $1.

Exercises and assignments

When the holder of an option wishes to take delivery of the under-lying interest on a particular option contract he may exercise his right to do so. For instance, you may have purchased a PGS August 40 call option. If Popular Gold has increased in price to, say, $45, you may wish to realize your profit. There are two ways of doing this. You may simply sell the call option on the stock exchange (the secondary market). Or you may choose to exercise your rights under the contract by actually purchasing the Popular Gold Stock shares at the $40 strike price stipulated by the call option contract — and subsequently sell the shares on the exchange at the market price of $45. When you choose the latter action, you are said to be exercis-ing your option. I'll have more to say about exercising your options in Chapter 6.

When you exercise your option, a broker acting as your agent will submit an exercise notice to either the exchange or the clearing cor-poration to initiate the purchase of the shares. Likewise, when the seller of a call option is requested to honour the terms of a contract, he is deemed to have been assigned his obligation. This in fact is the result of another party choosing to exercise his option. The per-son who has sold that option must deliver the appropriate amount of PGS shares to the investor who has exercised his option, at the stipulated exercise price. The shares must then be sold at this price regardless of the price they happen to be trading at on the exchange, and regardless of whether or not the person actually owns the shares he is required to sell. This of course could result in a dra-matic loss for the seller of the call option if the shares have risen far above the exercise price of the option. In any case, the seller will be debited the appropriate amount of stock which he must either bor-row from his broker or purchase on the exchange. When you sell options, you assume the risk of being assigned your obligations under the contract that you have written. You will see how to pre-pare for that risk in a later chapter.

American- or European-style options

Options are designated as either American- or European-style for exercise purposes. American-style exercise allows the holder to act or exercise his option at any time during the life of the contract. An American-style August option may be exercised at any time during the months preceding its exercise date, which is denoted as August.

European-style exercise only permits the holder of the option to exercise his contract when it actually expires. These different styles have important implications for the prices an option will trade at on the secondary market, and will be discussed in detail later in this book.

Currently in North America, equity options are deemed to be American-style exercise. Certain index options are denoted to be European-style exercise. The very popular Standard & Poor's 100 index option is American-style, while its cousin, the Standard & Poor's 500 is European-style. In Canada, the most heavily traded option is the Toronto 35 index option. It is also designated as European-style exercise.

Note that when exercising an index option it would be impractical to deliver a proportional amount of each underlying security covered by that specific index. Thus, index options are denoted as cash settled contracts. When one exercises or is assigned an index option, the value is calculated as a cash difference between the exercise price of the option and the closing level of the index on that particular day. This makes settlement of index options easy to manage for broker firms and the clearing corporations, but it also creates special risks for the index option investor. Readers may refer to Chapter 12 for a discussion of some of these risks.

Intrinsic and time value

If you exercise a PGS August 40 call option, you are purchasing 100 shares of Popular Gold Stock at $40. If the stock can be sold in the market at, say, $45 you will then realize a $5 profit. The difference between the market value of the underlying stock and the exercise price is known as the intrinsic value of the option. Of course, as we know from the example of obtaining insurance, you must usually pay a premium for the rights granted by an option contract. It would be somewhat foolhardy, and extremely risky, to grant someone these rights without receiving something in return. As a practical matter, you can rarely purchase an option in the market with an intrinsic value of $5 for exactly $5 — and certainly never for less. The PGS August 40 call option may cost $5.50 to purchase in the market when the stock is trading at $45. This difference between the intrinsic value of an option and its market price is known as the time value. The time value of PGS August 40 call option is $5.50 minus $5, or 50 cents.

The Relationship of Intrinsic Value, Time Value and Exercise Price for Two Options

PGS August 40 call

Price of underlying shares	$45
Exercise (strike) price of option	$40
Intrinsic value	$ 5
Price of call option contract	$5.50
Time value	50 cents

PGS August 45 call

Price of underlying shares	$45
Exercise (strike) price of option	$45
Intrinsic value	$ 0
Price of call option contract	50 cents
Time value	50 cents

TABLE III

In and out of the money

An option premium can be made up purely of intrinsic value, time value, or a combination of both. In the case of PGS August 40 call, the option is said to be in-the-money because the underlying stock is trading above the exercise price; it has some intrinsic value. If we change the prices somewhat, these concepts are more clearly seen.

PGS August 45 call option has no intrinsic value. If it were exercised, the stock purchased at $45 and subsequently sold in the market at $45, the net profit would be zero. However, it still has a value in the secondary market because there is still time for the underlying shares to increase in value. The price of the option over and above its intrinsic value is known as its time value. This option is also known as an at-the-money call because the exercise price is very near the price of the underlying stock. The call would be out-of-the-money if the stock was trading below the exercise price of the option.

In the case of a put option, which grants the holder the right to sell, the terms out-of-the-money and in-the-money apply in the opposite fashion. In order for a put option to be trading in-the-money, the stock price must be below the exercise price of the put. Conversely, to be out-of-the-money, the stock price must be above the exercise price of the put. Ask yourself this question: "Is it worth

---

How to Read Options Quotes in the Newspaper

Series		Bid	Close Ask	Last	Total option volume Volume	Open interest
Pop. Gold		$45 1/8			712	
Aug. 96	$40	5 1/4	$5 1/2	$5 1/4	114	642
	$40 P	0.45	0.60	0.50	232	453

Line 1: The class of option, Popular Gold Stock, is listed at the beginning of each set of quotes along with the closing price for that day's trading and the total volume of contracts (puts and calls) traded.

Line 2 & 3: Each series of option (puts and calls that trade on the same class of option) is listed along with its bid and ask, last sale, volume and open interest. The open interest, or the total number of options that have been written on that series, indicates the total number of contracts out-standing on that particular series of option. The more contracts outstand-ing, the easier it will be to execute a trade in that series.

Line 3: The option series are listed in ascending order if they have traded during that particular day. The "P" beside a series denotes a put; other-wise it is a call.

TABLE IV

more to sell the stock [by exercising the put] at the prevailing market price, or at the exercise price of the option?" If the exercise price is higher than the stock price, then the put is in-the-money; otherwise it is out-of-the-money.

Clearing corporations and margin requirements

A clearing corporation acts as the third party in transactions where an option is traded on an exchange. Its role is to issue and guarantee all listed options. This eliminates the risk of default by the seller of an option and creates a level playing field in the options market. After all, as we saw earlier, you would not want to buy insurance from a company that did not possess the resources to honour its ob-ligations in the event that one wanted to collect on a policy. A clear-ing corporation is able to guarantee these options because it requires a capital deposit from each of its members, mainly brokers, before it will allow them to conduct a public options business. By requiring a capital deposit, a clearing corporation ensures that it will have the resources to fulfill the obligations of the option con-tracts it issues. The broker, in turn, requires capital or margin from his clients who wish to enter into an option transaction. Margin is

Canadian Equity Options

Trading yesterday in Canadian equity options on the Toronto, Montreal, and Vancouver exchanges by the Canadian Derivatives Clearing Corp. P is a Put.

Five most active option classes

	Volume	Op Int
Barrick Gld	3016	26658
Diamond Fi	1410	23631
Kinross Gold	1040	3374
TSE 35	848	12380
BioChem Ph	393	19050

Stock Series		Close Bid	Ask	Last	Total Vol Vol	Tot Op Int Op Int
Abitibi-Price		**$21¾**			**180**	**5571**
Mar96	$22 p	0.70	0.90	0.45	60	249
	$24 p	2.30	2.55	2.25	10	78
Jun96	$20	2.35	2.60	2.65	25	145
	$22 p	1.45	1.70	1.25	30	56
	$24	0.55	0.80	0.70	25	160
Sep96	$20 p	0.95	1.20	0.75	10	60
	$22 p	1.80	2.05	1.80	20	70
Agnico Eagl		**$23½**			**15**	**966**
Mar96	$20	3.60	3.85	3.75	5	110
Sep96	$21	4.70	4.95	4.80	10	3
Air Canada		**$4.70**			**75**	**23424**
Jul96	$5	0.35	0.45	0.35	50	3905
Oct96	$4	0.55	0.70	0.55	5	55
	$5 p	0.50	0.60	0.50	20	50
Alberta Enr		**$24⅛**			**33**	**761**
Jun96	$23	1.75	1.95	2.10	33	78
Alcan		**$42⅛**			**113**	**9888**
Mar96	$40	2.35	2.60	2.60	5	45
	$42½	0.85	1.00	0.85	17	124
	$42½p	1.10	1.25	1.25	27	379
Apr96	$40 p	0.60	0.75	0.65	10	1373
	$42½	1.70	1.80	1.65	21	389
	$47½p	5⅜	5⅝	5⅝	3	23
Jul96	$37½	5¾	6	6¼	10	135
	$42½p	2.35	2.60	2.25	10	120
	$45	1.80	1.95	2.35	8	308
Jan97	$45	3.15	4.15	4.00	2	115
	$64 p	4.70	4.95	5	10	10
Jun96	$62	9⅛	9½	9⅛	2	22
	$64	8	8⅜	7⅝	4	219
Jan97	$32	34¼	34¾	33⅝	50	2683
	$40	27⅝	28⅛	27¾	235	829
	$60	15⅛	15⅝	16	7	36
Jan98	$50 p	6⅜	7	7⅛	1	20
	$65	16½	17⅛	16½	7	18
	$65 p	13⅛	13¾	13⅜	1	1
Biomira		**$7⅝**			**64**	**3445**
Mar96	$8	0.15	0.30	0.45	10	126
Apr96	$9	0.15	0.30	0.35	10	10
Jun96	$7 p	0.40	0.65	0.50	20	20
	$8	0.65	0.90	1.00	6	141
Sep96	$7 p	0.65	0.85	0.70	15	135
	$8 p	1.10	1.35	1.00	3	13
Bomb		**$20¼**			**49**	**5905**
Apr96	$20	1.00	1.25	1.20	6	89
	$21 p	1.05	1.30	1.05	10	49
	$22	0.40	0.65	0.65	5	55
Jul96	$21	1.25	1.50	1.50	21	538
Oct96	$20	2.25	2.50	2.50	4	121
Jan97	$14	7½	8	7½	3	138
Cambior		**$18½**			**75**	**3877**
Mar96	$19	0.50	0.75	0.70	20	95
Jul96	$18	2.35	2.60	2.75	5	124
	$18 p	1.30	1.55	1.40	5	151
	$21	1.10	1.35	1.35	20	140
Jan97	$16 p	0.70	1.20	0.70	20	70
	$18	3.05	3.55	3.25	5	189
Cameco		**$69**			**115**	**2101**
Apr96	$70	4.55	4.80	4.40	10	10
	$75	2.70	2.95	2.70	32	70
May96	$48	21⅛	21⅝	21¼	9	20
	$60	11	11½	11⅛	20	105
	$75	3.25	3.50	3.05	4	252
Nov96	$75	7⅛	7⅜	7⅜	40	40
Cdn Bd 2001		**$111.95**			**62**	**1518**
Mar96	$100	11.70	12.25	11.85	12	360
	$112p	0.50	0.75	0.50	50	384
	$32½	6	6½	6¼	17	449
	$35	4.05	4.35	4.15	132	3426
	$37½	2.15	2.55	2.55	132	3609
	$37½p	0.45	0.70	0.85	5	138
	$40	1.00	1.10	1.05	988	3274
Apr96	$35	4.50	4.75	4.70	10	99
	$37½	2.95	3.20	3.15	10	177
	$40	1.70	1.80	1.80	28	28
Jun96	$29	10¼	10¾	10⅝	5	107
	$32½	7⅜	7⅞	7½	10	92
	$35	5½	6	5⅞	10	121
	$35 p	0.80	1.05	0.80	5	100
	$40	2.60	3.00	2.50	3	112
Sep96	$35 p	1.00	1.25	1.25	5	85
	$37½	4.35	4.75	4.15	10	78
	$40	2.85	3.25	3.10	20	590
Dofasco Inc		**$20¼**			**50**	**2757**
Apr96	$20	0.80	1.05	0.85	50	50
Domtar Inc		**$10**			**12**	**5610**
Mar96	$10	0.25	0.30	0.25	2	38
May96	$11	0.25	0.50	0.45	10	477
Echo Bay		**$19¼**			**20**	**4343**
Apr96	$20	0.90	1.15	1.10	20	1266
Eicon Tech		**$10⅝**			**5**	**798**
Jul96	$12	0.80	1.00	0.75	5	65
Gaming		**$6**			**26**	**721**
Jun96	$6	1.20	1.45	1.20	10	102
	$7	0.75	0.90	0.75	6	36
	$9	0.30	0.45	0.30	10	10
Gandalf		**$19½**			**228**	**5149**
Mar96	$17	3.00	3.20	1.85	15	70
	$18	2.30	2.50	2.05	16	205
	$19	1.70	1.85	1.00	35	173
	$20	1.25	1.40	0.70	10	102
Apr96	$18	3.25	3.45	2.20	20	127
	$18 p	1.55	1.70	2.05	10	80
	$20	2.25	2.45	1.50	40	186
	$22½	1.40	1.55	1.00	10	164
Jul96	$16 p	2.00	2.20	2.40	10	170

SOURCE: THE GLOBE AND MAIL

TABLE V

required as a means of ensuring that clients can afford the transactions they wish to execute. Should large losses occur, there would otherwise be no assurance that investors could fulfill their obligations, and a financial default could result.

Margin requirements are uniform for the most part but can vary from broker to broker. The exchanges require a minimum amount of margin to be deposited for various trades. This has the effect of creating a level playing field since all clients are treated equally. But certain brokerage firms may request additional margin depending on the trading activity you wish to engage in. Clients should always consult their brokers to verify the amount of margin required for a transaction. Chapter 16 lists the current exchange minimum margin requirements for most listed option positions in Canada.

A clearing corporation also provides many other services for its members, such as the automatic exercise of options which are in-the-money when they expire. In the event that an investor has forgotten to exercise an option contract, a profit may needlessly go by the wayside. To prevent this from happening, the clearing corporation simply exercises all options that have a certain intrinsic value, on their expiry date. Thus, if you own a PGS August 40 call option when the underlying shares trade at $45, the clearing corporation will automatically exercise it for you on the third Saturday of August — ensuring you will realize your $5 profit. You may be surprised, on the following Monday morning, to learn that you now own 100 shares of Popular Gold Stock, but your broker will usually inform you of this event. In short, automatic exercise protects the profits of investors and simplifies the settlement process for its members. The clearing corporation will not automatically exercise all options with any value. The option must have at least a certain amount of intrinsic value before it will be exercised automatically.

At the time *Exploring Options* was written, the threshold for automatic exercise was 75 cents for equity options and 25 cents for index options. If an investor wishes to exercise an option that has an intrinsic value of less than the stated threshold for automatic exercise, he must submit an exercise notice to the clearing corporation stating his intention. This request is usually made through his broker.

In Canada, all listed stock and index options are cleared by Canadian Derivatives Clearing Corporation (CDCC). In the United States, it is The Options Clearing Corporation (OCC). CDCC and OCC are non-profit organizations. CDCC is owned by the three exchanges that trade options, Toronto, Montreal and Vancouver. OCC is a wholly owned subsidiary of the Chicago Board Options Exchange.

What's an Option Worth?

THE $64,000 QUESTION THAT all option traders face on a daily basis is whether an option is fairly priced. Does the market price accurately reflect the true value of a particular option? If you knew this for certain, it would be a simple matter to buy the underpriced options and sell the overpriced ones. This would grant you an enormous advantage over other investors. The reality is that it is impossible to know for certain what the value of an option should be. But it is possible to come to an understanding of why an option is trading at a certain price, and that is essential knowledge for every trader.

Six factors affecting the value of an option

Since we cannot determine the exact value an option should trade at in the market, we refer to its value as theoretical. There are six major factors which affect the theoretical value of an option:

- The price of the underlying asset;
- The exercise price of the option;
- The time remaining until the expiry date;
- The current interest rate, or risk-free rate of return;
- The dividend yield of the underlying security;
- The expected volatility of the underlying interest.

Of course, supply and demand as well as market sentiment are also factors in the value of an option. For instance, the theoretical value of an option may be $2 but because of supply and demand it may trade at $3 on the stock exchange. This may also be a result of market sentiment being either bullish or bearish. These occurrences are quite common, but we are dealing here with the abstract or theoretical value.

We have seen that the price of a Popular Gold Stock call option with an exercise price of $40 will be worth $5 when, at the expiry of that option, Popular Gold Stock trades at $45. We know this for the following reasons:

- There is no time left on the call option;
- There is no cost to carry the stock, because there is no time left to carry it for;
- There is no possibility of the call option changing price, because trading in that option has ceased;
- The final price of the option is known.

It is not nearly as simple to calculate the theoretical value of an option during the early days of its life. While the first five factors can easily be determined, the sixth, volatility, cannot. If we are dealing with a two-month option to purchase Popular Gold Stock at $40 per share we know:

- The current price of the stock;
- The exercise price, $40;
- The time remaining until expiry, 60 days;
- The current interest rate (the fact that it may change does not affect us at the moment);
- And the dividend to be paid on the stock, and whether one is due during the life of the option.

These factors can affect the prices of puts and calls in several ways. If the stock price goes higher, the price of the call option will rise and the price of the put option will fall. If the exercise price rises higher, the price of a call will be lower, and the price of a put will be higher. If there is more time remaining until the option expires, both call premiums and put premiums will be higher. If interest rates rise, call premiums will rise and put premiums will fall. If the dividend yield increases, call premiums will fall and put premiums will rise. Finally, if volatility rises, both call premiums and put premiums will rise.

These six factors are easy to define and relatively easy to understand. A call option to purchase the stock at $40 will have a different and higher price than a call to purchase the same security at $45. The fact that this difference is never exactly $5, except at expiry, may be a little confusing for the moment but this will be explained shortly. You will always know for certain the number of days remaining until the option expires. The more time remaining in the life of an option, the higher the price of that option. You will also know the current interest rate. This means that you can calculate the interest cost of funding the actual purchase of the underlying shares and holding the shares for the specified period of time.

Volatility

The only unknown factor here is the expected price change in the underlying stock. We are not talking about our personal forecast that the stock may reach a certain price. Unfortunately, the market does not carry much interest in our investment outlook. The key factor here is the probability of a given price movement occurring within a certain time frame. How likely is it that a price movement in the underlying stock will occur that will also affect the premium of the option? The greater the likelihood of a large price movement, the greater the premium of the option will be.

Volatility is a somewhat different factor than the others that we have examined. It is a conceptual rather than an empirical element. The volatility of an option is concerned with the expected price movement of the underlying security. Volatility is not concerned with the price of the underlying security, per se. Nor is it concerned with the direction of the expected price movement. Volatility is the probability of a given price movement in the underlying stock occurring within a certain time frame. Any calculation which involves a forecast or expectation cannot be considered, by definition, to be statistically precise. Volatility reflects the range of price changes that an underlying stock is expected to experience during the life of an option. If a stock is known to commonly experience price swings of several dollars per day, then an option on that stock will command a relatively higher price than a comparatively stable stock. When the volatility of a security increases, the premiums on both the puts and calls increase.

How do the professionals deal with this unexpected, unknown quantity when they are trading options? They observe price volatility from a historical perspective. You can identify the historical trading range of a stock and apply a probability factor to that range. Statisticians refer to this as the normal distribution of prices. Students of statistics will note that a normal distribution is graphically represented as a bell curve. If a stock has never traded outside of a specific range, the probability of it doing so in the future is extremely low. The opposite is true of a stock that routinely trades in wider ranges. This trading range is defined by statisticians as a standard deviation. Simply stated, the standard deviation is a percentage amount in which certain cases will occur over a period of time. If, for example, one standard deviation is $10, then statistics indicate that two out of every three price occurrences should be within that $10 range.

The volatility of an option is represented by a percentage figure that is equivalent to one standard deviation. The standard deviation can be calculated by taking the historical volatility as a percentage figure and multiplying it by the stock price. Thus, the value of a one-standard deviation move for a stock trading at $50 with a historical volatility of 30 per cent would be $15. A two-standard deviation move would be $30, and so on. For pricing purposes, the volatility of an option is usually taken from the previous two months' trading of the underlying stock. The next step is to use the volatility figure to compute the theoretical price of the option. Thus, the actual price of an option is said to be implying a certain volatility according to its actual market premium. You do not know for certain if this volatility figure will in fact prove to be accurate in the future because, by definition, the future is unknown to us.

Entire books have been written on the topic of volatility and the mathematics are far too in-depth for the purposes of this book. But I included the above description to illustrate that the calculation of an option premium is not an accident of the market. It is not produced by monkeys at a typewriter. There is a rhyme and reason to the resulting price of an option. The first breakthrough in this field came with the development of the Black-Scholes pricing model. For option traders, the Black-Scholes is the trading equivalent to Darwin's *Origin of Species*.

The Black-Scholes pricing model

Two University of Chicago professors, Fischer Black and Myron Scholes, formulated a method of calculating the theoretical price of an option by taking the known variables we identified earlier, and calculating an implied volatility figure. The result was the Black-Scholes pricing model: the single most widely used tool for calculating the theoretical price of an option. The original model was designed to calculate the value of a European-style option on some underlying asset which does not pay a dividend. It is reprinted below for calculus enthusiasts, but, to say the least, it is much easier to use in practice with a computer to do the work for you.

The Black-Scholes Pricing Model

Theoretical option price $= pN\left(d_1\right) - se^{-rt}N\left(d_2\right)$

where $\quad d_1 = \dfrac{\ln\left(\dfrac{p}{s}\right) + \left(r + \dfrac{v^2}{2}\right)t}{v\sqrt{t}}$

$\quad\quad\quad d_2 = d_1 - v\sqrt{t}$

The variables are:

p = Stock price
s = Strike price
t = Time remaining until expiration, expressed as a per cent of a year
r = Current risk-free interest rate
v = Volatility measured by annual standard deviation
$\ln$ = Natural logarithm
$N(x)$ = Cumulative normal density function

CHART I

Although the mathematics look intimidating, the model has quite an easy application. For instance, if you were to supply the six known quantities — stock price, exercise price, dividend yield, time to expiry, current interest rate and the price of the option — you would, by default, be supplied with a volatility rating as the last and missing element when the option premium is input and the calculation is performed. You would then see the volatility that the market price of an option is implying.

This exercise is not intended to merely satisfy the predilections of the intellectually curious; it has an important practical application. You can compare the implied volatility of the option to the historical volatility of the underlying security. The volatility figures of stocks are readily available from the statistics divisions of the stock exchanges on which they are listed.

Armed with the historical volatility numbers on the underlying stock, you can see if an option implies a volatility which is consistent with the historical volatility of its underlying stock. You can see if the volatility is too high or too low. In short, you would know if an option is fairly priced in historical terms. If the volatility comparison shows that an option is overpriced, sell it; if it is theoretically underpriced, buy it.

There are, in fact, many investors who trade the market using volatility factors alone. They simply chart the historical volatility of a security, or the market as a whole, and sell when the volatility is high and buy when it is low. As a practical matter, even if you are contemplating the purchase of stock, it is prudent to be aware of the historical volatility of a given security — especially if you are making a somewhat speculative purchase.

A warning about volatility

The average options trader should take special care to examine the underlying security when there appears to be a drastic change in its volatility. There is usually a good reason for this change. It could be based on rumour or fundamentals. If the outcome of a major lawsuit is due during the life of the option, then that could easily be the cause of an increase in volatility. This takes us back to the earlier notes about fundamentals. Make sure that there isn't some hidden surprise in the underlying security that is causing a sudden change in the volatility of the option. It is rare that the market does not factor in all of the known risk. Don't presume that you have spotted some anomaly that the market has discounted. The market rarely makes this type of mistake. My own view is that since there are rooms full of traders with high-powered computers around the world who watch the market constantly, how can I presume to know something which they do not?

This has been a relatively simplified discussion on volatility and its impact on option pricing. Volumes have been written on the subject. We will be looking at volatility, from a practical point of view, in the chapters on option strategies.

Remember to evaluate the underlying security

We refer to the theoretical value of an option because it is impossible to determine an option's exact value. Five of these factors are easy to determine. The sixth factor, the expected volatility of the underlying security, can be calculated using the Black-Scholes pricing model for options. By comparing the implied volatility of an option to the historical viability of its underlying security, you can learn whether an option is fairly priced in historical terms. This information will help you decide whether to buy or sell a particular option. However, volatility pales in comparison to the importance of evaluating the security underlying an option. In fact, it should only be considered after you have completed your research and have made a decision to buy or sell a security. Only then will you have the knowledge that will allow you to buy or sell an option. Now that you know the components of option pricing, let's look at how the options market uses this information.

CHAPTER 4

The Logic of Options Markets

YOU MAY HAVE HEARD THAT options are efficiently priced, or that the options market is efficient. Why this is so requires some explanation. In the previous chapter you learned why an option trades at a particular price. In this chapter you will learn how that option comes to trade at a particular price. Let's look at an example of the dynamics of option pricing in the marketplace to illustrate how the intrinsic value of an option maintains a certain relationship to its underlying stock. You will see how market-maker arbitrage and interest rates affect option pricing.

Stocks and options

Purchasing a stock has somewhat the same potential for profit as a call option, with one important difference — the premium you must pay for that option. The risk potential is also somewhat different. Theoretically, the stock purchaser risks his entire investment. While the call option purchaser also risks his entire investment, he paid a much smaller amount of money for the call option. And the risk of losing his investment is subject only to the lifetime of the option. An option will expire worthless if it is not sold or exercised before its expiry date. There is no predetermined lifetime to the purchase of stock.

Chart II illustrates the profit line of stock ownership. The main characteristic of the risk and reward of stock ownership is unlimited profit. The maximum loss occurs if the stock declines to zero. The vertical axis measures the profit or loss potential of a position. The horizontal axis measures the price of the stock. The horizontal line dividing the centre of the graph represents the purchase price of the stock, $25. The diagonal line represents the profit or loss for a given stock price movement. Where the diagonal line crosses the horizontal line is the break-even point. When the stock

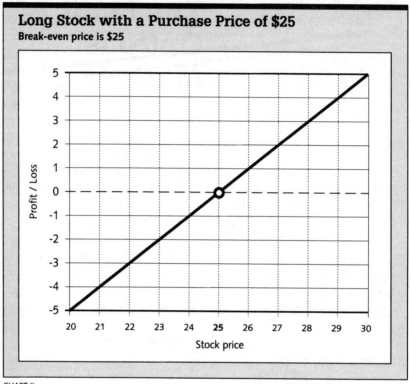

Long Stock with a Purchase Price of $25
Break-even price is $25

CHART II

declines to $22, the investor suffers a $3 loss. Likewise, when the stock advances to $28, the investor realizes a $3 profit.

Now compare Chart II to Chart III, which illustrates the profit line of a call option. Here the call option premium is $2 and the exercise price is $25. The similarity between a long call and owning stock is directional. The market bias for both positions is bullish. They both profit when the stock advances. The theoretical potential for profit is unlimited, but the call buyer does not profit until the stock advances beyond $27 because of the initial $2 premium required to purchase the call. The major benefit of owning the call instead of the underlying stock is the limited loss facing the call holder in the event of a decline in the stock price. This loss is limited to the cost of the option. The profit/loss line in Chart III never drops below $2. The major benefit of stock ownership over call option ownership is the absence of the need to time the invest-

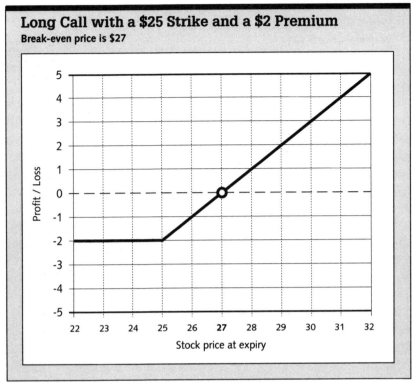

Long Call with a $25 Strike and a $2 Premium
Break-even price is $27

CHART III

ment. The stock will not expire and can be held over the course of a much longer period of time. The call option has a limited lifetime.

Chart IV is the profit graph of a put option. You can see that the graph is a mirror image of the profit/loss line for the long call shown in Chart III. Again the maximum loss is the cost of the premium, but the profit is also limited to the maximum amount the stock can decline minus the amount of the put option. In this case, the stock price can decline to zero dollars. Therefore, the maximum profit of the position is $23, or $25 minus $0 minus $2. A short seller would profit in a similar manner if a stock declined, but he would also be exposed to the risk of an unlimited advance in the price of the stock.

There are other differences to owning a call instead of stock. Stock may carry a dividend, stock usually requires a significantly greater cash outlay, and stock usually grants the owner a vote in the affairs of the company at the annual meeting. While a long call posi-

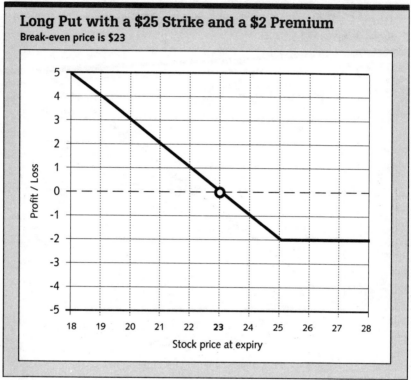

Long Put with a $25 Strike and a $2 Premium
Break-even price is $23

CHART IV

tion and a long stock position are not quite the same, it is possible to create the equivalent to a stock position using options. To make the option position equivalent, you must do two things. You must find a way to pay for the premium of the call option, so your break-even point is the same on the profit graph for both positions. And you must find a way to replicate the loss created when stock declines, which removes the limited loss characteristic of the call option. Why you would want to do this will become clear shortly. The easiest way to accomplish both tasks is to sell a put option at the same time you purchase a call. If you simultaneously purchase a call and sell a put you can reproduce the profit/loss potential of owning stock.

First, let's look at the profit graph of a short put option, Chart V. Again the put premium is $2 and the exercise price and stock price are $25. The short put is the mirror image of the long put. The maximum profit is the amount the seller receives for the put. It is real-

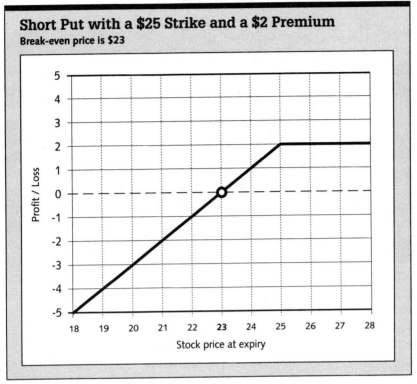

Short Put with a $25 Strike and a $2 Premium
Break-even price is $23

CHART V

ized when the stock trades at $25 or higher at expiry. But the profit is also limited to the amount of the premium received for selling the put, or $2. The maximum loss is realized when the stock declines to zero; and this is offset slightly by the $2 premium. Since the put seller is obligated to purchase the stock at $25, the maximum potential loss is $25 minus $0 minus $2, or $23. The break-even point is $23, the exercise price minus the premium received.

Now return to the long call and superimpose it over the short put. This creates Chart VI. In this chart, the profit line runs from the bottom left corner of the graph to the upper right corner. In fact, the profit line is identical to that of a long stock position. Note that with the price paid for the call option equal to the amount received for selling the put option, the break-even point returns to $25, or the exercise price and stock price in our example.

Assuming there are no dividends on the stock, this position is equivalent to owning stock with one major difference — the cost of

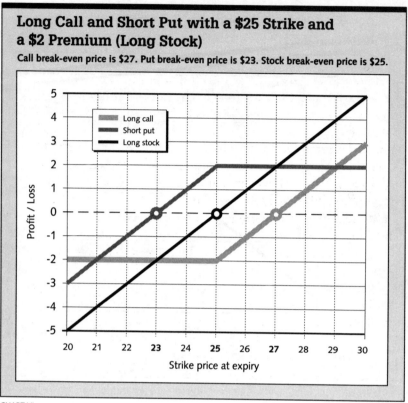

Long Call and Short Put with a $25 Strike and a $2 Premium (Long Stock)

Call break-even price is $27. Put break-even price is $23. Stock break-even price is $25.

CHART VI

carrying the underlying stock. If you could simultaneously buy a call and sell a put for a net cost of $0, then you would have created a long stock position without the need to invest the cost of purchasing the stock. You would avoid the loss of interest on the funds represented by the purchase price of the underlying interest. By buying a call, selling a put and buying a T-bill, you would be considerably further ahead than the stock purchaser. This represents an arbitrage opportunity, and the reason that options markets are efficient is a function of arbitrage.

Arbitrage

Arbitrage is the ability to simultaneously buy and sell something at a profit without incurring any risk. In the early days of stock markets, traders would purchase a security on one exchange and sell it on another to take advantage of price disparities between the markets. A stock might trade between $45 and $45.125 on the New

York Stock Exchange, and between $45.25 and $45.375 on the London Stock Exchange. The arbitrage trader would then sell the stock at $45.25 in London and simultaneously purchase it in New York for $45.125, guaranteeing a profit of 12.5 cents. The arbitrageur would continue this trading until the prices in New York and London were back to the same level. The act of selling in one market and buying in another has the effect of pushing prices back in line. The advent of modern technology and communications has eliminated most arbitrage in the classic definition of the term, because traders can easily view other markets and instantly execute trades around the world. However, the concept of arbitrage is actively at work in the option market every day.

Think back to our example of the intrinsic value of the Popular Gold Stock August 40 call option. The option was trading at $5.50 when its intrinsic value was $5. If for some reason the price of the option fell to $4.50 when the stock was trading at $45, you would have an arbitrage opportunity. It would be a simple matter to sell 100 shares of the stock in the market at $45, purchase the call option at $4.50 and subsequently exercise the call option, thereby purchasing 100 shares at $40. This would flatten out the stock position and guarantee you a profit of 50 cents a share, or $50.

In fact, the possibility of this type of trade ensures that the price of the option will never trade below its intrinsic value. This is largely due to the fact that equity options are American-style exercise. This allows the holder of the option to exercise at any time during the life of the contract, and to realize any profits from disparities such as these.

If the options were European-style exercise, then they could not be exercised until expiry. Because of this, there are cases where an option actually trades at a price below its intrinsic value, or at a discount, until it reaches its expiry date. In these cases, the option actually "matures" to its real intrinsic value. The main reason for this is the inability of the holder of a European-style option to exercise it and immediately capitalize on any price differences. This will happen at times when an option becomes so deep-in-the-money that it loses its leverage and is merely a surrogate for the underlying interest. This is usually the case with European-style index options that are $50 or more in-the-money.

Synthetic positions and conversions

You have seen that an equivalent stock position can be created using combinations of puts and calls. Market-makers in the options market make it their business to take advantage of these arbitrage opportunities. This ensures that a certain pricing relationship will always exist between the underlying stock and the price of the puts and calls. Market-makers look for the opportunity to buy these calls and sell these puts at prices which will replicate the long stock position. Once they are able to do this, market-makers will then execute a sale of the stock at the same time. When they add to this position by selling the stock, they lock in a risk-free position. The main reason this type of three-tiered trade is profitable for market-makers is because they receive interest on the proceeds of the short stock sale.

But before market-makers will do so, the profit they lock in must exceed the return that can be made on some other risk-free investment, such as a T-bill. Otherwise why would they bother to execute such a complicated transaction when there was such a simple alternative available. This is essentially how interest rates affect the pricing of options. Interest rates define the positions that represent an arbitrage opportunity for market-makers.

Table VI illustrates some equivalent positions in the marketplace using options. Market-makers use this knowledge on a daily basis to exploit opportunities in the options market. They are constantly watching for prices which will allow them to buy one position and sell its synthetic equivalent at a risk-free profit. A position is defined as risk-free when a change in the price of the underlying security will not produce a profit or loss. It is not the business of most market-makers to make long-term investments that require them to forecast the direction a stock will take. They seek to eliminate this risk while still ensuring a profit for themselves. They are able to do this because their transaction costs are very small. They are merely required to pay the exchange clearing fees. These transactions are generally prohibitive to the average investor because of commission fees. The average investor will also find that his broker will not pay him interest on the proceeds of any short sales. This is largely because of the cost of borrowing the stock.

The most common type of investment used by market-makers is to either buy the underlying stock and sell the option equivalent, or sell the underlying stock and buy its option equivalent. The former

Market Positions and Their Synthetic Equivalents

Position	Synthetic equivalent
Long stock	Long call + short put
Short stock	Short call + long put
Long call	Long stock + long put
Short call	Short stock + short put
Long put	Short stock + long call
Short put	Long stock + short call

TABLE VI

is known as a conversion because you convert the stock into an equivalent synthetic position. The goal is to be able to obtain a price for the call you sell which will offset the cost of both the purchase price of the put and the cost of carrying the stock. If the underlying stock has a dividend due during the life of the position it will also affect the carrying cost by reducing it according to the dividend payment. The remaining carrying cost is defined by the amount you would receive if the purchase price of the stock was reinvested in an interest-bearing investment.

The opposite strategy of selling the stock short and buying synthetic long stock is known as a reconversion. In this case, the premium received for selling the put plus the amount received by investing the proceeds of the short stock (less any dividends) should exceed the amount of the cost of the call. This locks in a profit.

Delta

The final concept I would like to discuss is the delta. The delta is a byproduct of the Black-Scholes pricing model. While volatility is concerned with the expected price movement in the underlying security, the delta defines how much money you can expect to make if the underlying stock moves in the direction you expect it to. The delta, or hedge ratio, is the anticipated amount of change in the price of an option for every one-point change in the price of the underlying security. In other words, the delta represents the amount an option will change in price if the underlying security changes in price by one point. If an option has a delta of 0.5, you could expect the option to increase by 50 cents for every dollar the stock increased. The delta of a call option is expressed as a positive figure, while the delta of a put option is expressed as a negative. The delta of long stock is 1.00, and the delta of short stock is -1.00. Thus, the delta of a call is expressed as a value between 1.00 and zero, and the delta of a put is expressed as a value between zero and -1.00.

Professionals use delta in a slightly different manner from the average investor. The small investor merely makes a mental picture of the price an option should advance to if the underlying stock advances to his forecast price, based upon the current delta of the stock. Professionals and market-makers use their knowledge of delta to profit from an option position without being exposed to a price movement in the underlying security. Remember, a market-maker can readily put on a risk-free position by buying or selling the underlying stock and executing its synthetic opposite in the options market. However, these pure trading arbitrage situations are not always readily available even to the market-maker. To avoid directional risk in an options position, market-makers must look elsewhere for profitable positions. And to make a position free from directional risk, they must create a position which is delta neutral.

The following example represents the delta of the well-known covered write strategy:

delta of long stock	+1.00
delta of a short at-the-money call	-0.50
net delta risk	+0.50

This is not enough for market-makers, however, because if the stock declines they will suffer a loss. Remember, they are not investors and have no interest in the prospects of a particular stock for future advancement. They seek to eliminate the directional risk, or delta risk, that is represented in the above example as a net of +0.50. The above position is net long one-half of a delta point. To eliminate this they can simply purchase one at the money put, which has an approximate delta of -0.50, creating this position:

delta of long stock	+1.00
delta of a short call	-0.50
delta of a long put	-0.50
net delta risk	0.00

Ideally, they will have executed the above trades at a profit which will return a yield greater than the prevailing interest rate. If not, then why not simply purchase a risk-free investment such as a T-bill? But as I said, these trades are not always readily available in

such a neat easy-to-execute package. Thus, an alternative must be
sought. Let's return to the covered write example and adjust it
somewhat:

delta of long stock	+1.00
delta of two, short at-the-money calls	-1.00
net delta risk	0.00

Those of you who have skipped ahead to the advanced strategy
chapter will recognize this as a ratio write, the writing of more options than are covered by a corresponding stock or call position.
Now the position is again delta neutral but without the purchase of
the put. It could also be made to be delta neutral by selling an out-
of-the-money call (delta of -0.20) combined with the sale of an in-
the-money call (delta of -0.80). In fact, there are various ways of
accomplishing the same position with puts and calls merely by
totalling the delta of the combined position. The key is to receive an
overall credit for the position and avoid exposing yourself to the
direction of the market.

Portfolio insurance

In the above ratio write example, the position is exposed to a significant risk of the underlying security advancing in price because
both of the calls are not covered. There is the further risk of an increase in the volatility of the options that have been sold. Let's return to our example and assume that the underlying stock advances
by $2 so that the options are now slightly in-the-money. The delta
of the two short calls that were sold would also increase giving the
position an overall negative delta. To make the position delta
neutral would require that you purchase the underlying security
(positive delta) in an amount equal to the increase in the delta of the
calls. If the stock again returned to its original price, the position
would have an overall positive delta and another adjustment would
have to be made, such as selling some of the long stock position. In
fact, this process requires many adjustments over the lifetime of a
strategy. This strategy is known as portfolio insurance because of
the constant adjustments required to protect the stock. This osten-
sibly removes the risk of a major loss. It is also a "buy high, sell
low" strategy. The intent is to capture the cash flow of the option
premiums, as well as any dividends or interest payments that may
be due on the portfolio during the lifetime of the option positions,
without incurring the risk of market direction.

Portfolio insurance was once a popular method employed by fund managers, but it fell out of favour after the 1987 stock market crash. During the crash, the rapid decline in stock prices was accelerated by portfolio insurers selling large amounts of securities in order to remain delta neutral. Of course, they had tremendous difficulty keeping up with the pace of the market decline and substantial losses occurred. The situation was exacerbated by the very fact that fund managers were selling so much stock, causing the market to fall further and further by their very actions. Portfolio insurers had little alternative but to sell stocks during the crash because of various difficulties in the options and futures markets. As a practical matter, the alternative tactic of selling index calls or futures, or buying index puts, was not viable because of delays in market openings and because of position limit rules that legally limited the number of options or futures an individual could buy or sell. I do not mean to condemn delta hedging or portfolio insurance. One of the main problems at the time of the crash was that virtually everyone was using this strategy. This lack of diversity led to instability in the marketplace. This was finally uncovered by the Brady Commission which reported that 30 per cent of all equity transactions on the New York Stock Exchange that Monday were done by portfolio insurers.

Summary
Options markets work to maintain the relationship between the value of an option and its underlying security. In particular, arbitrage and interest rates have a marked effect on options pricing. In the next chapter you will get a closer look at the dynamics of the time value of an option.

CHAPTER 5

The Life Span of an Option

TIME VALUE IS ONE OF THE two essential components of an option's value. You know that options lose some of their value over the course of time. But before you can consider buying a call or a put it is essential to understand the relationship of time to the value of an option. You must also understand how the passing of time will affect an option's price. This knowledge is fundamental to deciding what options to buy or sell.

When there is no time remaining on the life of an option, the price of the option will be its intrinsic value. And if the option has no intrinsic value left, the price of the option will be zero. Chart VII traces the life of a typical 90-day call option which is trading at-the-money. The chart is for illustration purposes only and does not necessarily show the exact path of the decay of a particular 90-day option. The decay chart of an option will vary depending on the option's underlying interest. This is because of the different volatilities of various securities and the amount of time value each has in their premiums. The chart assumes that the option is exactly at-the-money, so that the option has no intrinsic value. The chart also assumes that the other factors affecting the option's price, such as the price of the underlying security, remain relatively stable.

When to buy or sell an option

This call begins with its maximum time value when it has 90 days left to expiry. Note that because the exercise price of the option is equal to the market price of the stock, or at-the-money, the price is composed entirely of time value. As time advances, the number of days remaining to expiry and the value of the option both decline until they reach zero. But the decline in value does not occur in a straight line. Chart VII illustrates one of the most fundamental concepts of options trading: The rate of time decay accelerates as the expiry date of the option approaches.

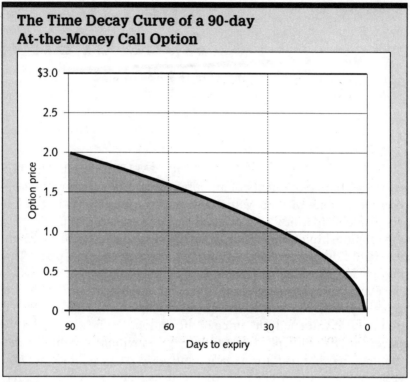

The Time Decay Curve of a 90-day At-the-Money Call Option

Option price / Days to expiry

CHART VII

Time works against the purchaser of an option. This makes it necessary to correctly forecast a price movement within the lifetime of a call or put. Your option can easily lose its value and expire prior to the underlying stock experiencing a directional move that would have been profitable. The time decay chart shows us that an option will not lose its value as quickly during the early days of its lifetime as it will later on. Armed with this knowledge it is easy to see that for options buyers the best investment is the one that has the longer lifetime, but not necessarily the longest. An option with a longer lifetime will not lose its value as quickly as a shorter dated option. Conversely, the best option to sell is the one with the shorter lifetime, because of the faster erosion of its time value.

My experience has shown that most individual investors choose to purchase options which have the lowest premiums. They do this for fear of losing too much money if their forecast for the stock is wrong, and also to obtain the most leverage. Oddly enough, an investor usually stands to lose less by purchasing the longer-term option even though the cost is higher. The reason, of course, is the slower rate of time decay on the longer-term option.

Making the time decay curve work for you

For example, using our time decay chart, notice the difference between the price of a 90-day option compared to the price of a 30-day option. There is a drastic drop in value from the 60-day option to the 30-day option. But there is a relatively modest drop in value from a 90-day option to a 60-day option. An investor who wanted to purchase a 30-day call on a certain security would actually be better off purchasing a 60- or even a 90-day call and only hold it for 30 days. This is true especially when an investor's forecast turns out to be incorrect and the stock does not perform. The owner of the 30-day call would lose his entire investment, while the purchaser of the 60-day call would lose only 40 per cent of his investment. In other words, if your forecast calls for a certain movement in a stock within a 30-day time period, the safest action would be to purchase a 90-day option and sell it when there are only 60 days left. You will still have purchased an option for 30 days, but it will probably not decline to zero if your directional forecast on the underlying stock turns out to be incorrect.

The sacrifice the longer-term option buyer makes for this bit of security is a certain amount of leverage. The shorter-term buyer will be able to leverage a great deal more stock since he will be able to purchase more options. At the least, he will be using less capital for control of the stock than the longer-term buyer. To be fair, most option buyers are attracted to the market because of this leverage factor. Why give up leverage when this is what brought you to the options market in the first place? The point to consider here is the balance you seek in your investments: the amount of risk you take with the capital you have for investment. It is riskier to invest in a shorter-term vehicle because you have less time to be proven right in the market. If you are pursuing a high-leverage investment program such as short-term, out-of-the-money option purchases, then money management will be an extremely important factor. Without a great deal of skill, or luck, you will deplete your funds very quickly.

The rate of decline in the premium of an option is known as the theta. Just like the delta, you can calculate the theta of an option.

Appendix 1 provides a more detailed discussion of this and other statistical concepts. In options pricing theory, these concepts are affectionately known as the Greeks. Right now, let's look at strategies for buying and selling puts and calls.

CHAPTER 6

Buying Calls and Puts

AN OPTION STRATEGY IS A
tool that you can use to build your overall investment strategy.
Learning these strategies will help you understand the relationships
among various option positions and the risk and reward offered by
each. In this chapter, we will look at the basics of buying calls and
puts. You will learn the market bias of both strategies, their use in
specific market situations and possible alternative strategies. I don't
believe that you must always use options in your investment
strategy. After all, there are times when it is more advantageous to
buy the underlying stock instead of buying a call option. The important factor is to be able to recognize when a particular option
strategy meets your investment objectives.

Risk and reward

The concept of risk and reward constantly appears whenever options are being discussed. I am not sure why it doesn't appear with
similar frequency in discussions of other investment tools. Risk and
reward is the most basic relationship between the quality of the investment and its potential return. When you buy a T-bill, you know
the risk and the reward. The investment is risk-free and it will have
a fixed yield. When you purchase a stock, you risk losing your entire investment, but your reward is theoretically unlimited. However, the theoretical risk and reward of buying stock paints a stark
picture for most investors. Most investors don't really believe that
they are risking a 100 per cent loss when they purchase a blue chip
stock. Nor do they believe that the potential profit is quadruple the
current price of that stock.

Wise investors assign a stock certain price perimeters, based
upon the performance of many factors such as earnings and
economic climate. After creating these perimeters, they assign the
stock to a range, or a risk-reward profile, in which they expect it to

trade over a certain period of time. This exercise is something that you should always do when you analyze an option strategy. The purpose of this is not only to make you aware of what you have at stake, but also to help you decide whether the investment is worthwhile. Is the reward worth the risk?

Recently, a friend of mine was contemplating a trade that involved using a conservative, neutral strategy on an extremely volatile stock. He calculated that assuming the stock did not decline by more than 25 per cent during the course of seven business days he would earn a 5 per cent profit. The return was attractive and the risk of the stock declining so drastically seemed low. At first glance, this scenario appeared to be acceptable from a risk and reward point of view. But in the stock market you must always ask, "Why is the market offering such a high return?" High returns, such as 5 per cent in one week, are only available on high-risk investments. In this particular case, after doing some checking on the stock, I learned that the company was involved in a lawsuit that could dramatically affect its share price. Furthermore, the suit was to be decided prior to the expiry of the options my friend wanted to trade. Analysts were predicting that if the company lost the suit the shares would decline by as much as 40 per cent. My friend would be taking on a tremendous amount of risk in order to profit by a small amount.

You might argue that he would turn a profit if the company won its lawsuit. There is nothing wrong with this thinking, but there is something wrong with the return on his investment. For that amount of risk, my friend should have expected a tremendous return on his investment. His choice of strategy limited his profit but did not control his risk. There are several strategies that would have been more appropriate to my friend in such a situation. One strategy would have been to simply buy a call option. The point is to select the strategy that best controls your risks, while offering you a satisfactory return on your investment if your forecast turns out to be correct. If you know what the risks and rewards are, you will be able to select an appropriate strategy. To put it in the simplest terms, if your investment goal is long-term growth with income, then purchasing a blue chip stock that pays a dividend is probably the right strategy for you.

Buying calls

Buying calls is a bullish strategy. You buy calls when you expect that a particular security, or the market as a whole, will advance. Call options have their own set of benefits and risks. A call has the potential for theoretically unlimited profit, while the potential loss of a call is limited to the premium paid for the option. As well, the holder of a call has the right to choose when to exercise his option. On the other hand, a call has a limited lifetime, and time works against the buyer of a call. More importantly, the call buyer risks losing all of his limited investment.

Remember the profit graph for a long call shown in Chart III; that graph assumes an option with an exercise price of $25 and a premium of $2. At expiry, that option will have a value equal to the amount by which the stock price exceeds the exercise price. The option holder is under no obligation to take any action according to the definition and terms of the contract. The holder's loss is limited to the premium paid for the call — $2. The maximum loss will occur when the stock trades at $25 or lower at expiry. Even if the stock declines to zero, the loss cannot change and will still only be $2. The option has a theoretically unlimited profit potential since there is no limit to the price the underlying stock might climb to. The actual profitability can be calculated like this:

The stock price at expiry	$xx
Minus the exercise price	$25
Minus the premium	$2

The call purchaser is basically banking on two things: the direction of the underlying stock; and the time period in which the price change will take place. He is also anticipating that the stock will move in an amount that will be greater than the premium paid for the call, if he plans to hold the option to expiry. In the above example, the price of the underlying stock must move beyond the break-even point of $27 before the option will be profitable. However, in the early life of the option this may not be necessary in order to realize a profit. If the underlying stock starts trading at a higher price, the price of the call option will also be higher. As we discussed in Chapter 4, this relationship is known as the delta. If you were to buy a call option with an exercise price of $40 when the underlying stock trades at $30, you would still profit if the stock were to experience a certain price move in the early life of the option. The reason for this is that the price has moved before there has been a significant amount of time elapsed from the life of the option. The higher the stock moves in relationship to the exercise price of the call, the higher the call premium.

Choosing a call option

Choosing which call option to purchase depends upon many factors. Beginning with your investment objectives and your price forecast of the underlying stock, these choices can be narrowed somewhat. Obviously, if your objective is to get rich quick, you will choose the highest risk and highest reward investment. Your choice will be the same if you expect a stock's price to double or triple in a very short period of time. For most of us, neither of these are the case. Truly, they are somewhat unrealistic. Let us assume that you seek moderate capital gains with a small amount of risk. In order to choose the best call or put to buy we must revisit that mysterious concept of leverage.

The greatest amount of leverage is achieved when you have invested the smallest amount of capital and control, or are exposed to, the largest amount of stock. This is most easily done by purchasing out-of-the-money call options. Conversely, the least leverage is achieved when purchasing in-the-money call options. For example, assume that a particular stock is trading at $25 and you are anticipating a price advance. The prices of 30-, 60- and 90-day calls are illustrated in Table VII.

The maximum leverage is achieved through the purchase of the 30-day call with an exercise price of $30. The 30-day call with a strike price of $30 is only 6.25 cents compared to the 90-day call which is trading at 25 cents. That means you would be able to buy four times as many of the 30-day calls as you would of the 90-day calls. Or consider the 90-day call with a strike price of $20 trading at $5.50. For the purchase of one of these calls, you could buy 88 of the 30-day calls with a strike price of $30. Using the same amount of capital, you can choose to control either 100 shares or 8,800 shares. That's quite a spectrum to choose from.

To illustrate the effect of this leverage, let's suppose that the stock advances to $31 within the 30-day time frame. At expiry, the 90-day call with a strike of $20 would be worth $1,000. The 30-day call with a strike of $30 would be worth $8,800. An investment of $550 turned into $8,800 with a 24 per cent move in the underlying stock, over the course of 30 days. The investment in the 30-day call

The Leverage Afforded by 30-, 60- and 90-Day Call Options

Stock price = $25

Strike price	30-day term	60-day term	90-day term
$20.00	$5.125	$5.375	$5.500
$22.50	$2.875	$3.375	$3.750
$25.00	$0.375	$0.625	$0.825
$27.50	$0.125	$0.250	$0.500
$30.00	$0.0625	$0.125	$0.250

TABLE VII

options yielded a return of 1,760 per cent in one month's time. That is leverage.

In the real world, you rarely expect such fantastic fortune and merely seek to enjoy profits that reward you for the risk you assume. Looking at Table VII of available options, the 90-day option with an exercise price of $25 offers good leverage for the risk you would assume. Don't forget that you risk losing your entire investment. You do not need an exceptional price move to capitalize on your investment. An 8 per cent advance in the price of the stock over the course of a three-month period is not an altogether unlikely forecast, particularly if you are bullish. If this advance should occur then you would have doubled your investment. The calls cost 87.5 cents and would be worth $2 by expiry, when the stock had advanced to $27. This is what I deem to be acceptable leverage for a call purchase. The option will have doubled in value during its lifetime if your forecast on the underlying stock was correct. This allows you to fit your forecast to your money management scheme. Remember, the money management approach discussed in Chapter 1 requires that you only invest 10 per cent of your risk capital at any given time. The life span of the 90-day option will also usually be sufficient time for the expected price advance to come to pass.

Based upon the above example, you will find that it is usually the at-the-money options that fulfill these criteria. You will also note an additional benefit of choosing the 90-day option as opposed to the 30- or 60-day option. After 60 days have elapsed, your option will still have a value of approximately 37.5 cents, assuming no price movement. Thus, even though your forecast may only be for a

60-day period it is still better to purchase the 90-day call and plan to hold it only for 60 days. If you had purchased the 60-day call you would have lost your entire investment. By purchasing the 90-day call you have lost only the difference between the 60- and 90-day calls instead of the entire cost of the 60-day call, or 50 cents instead of 62.5 cents.

The downside to buying the 90-day call is that you must put more capital at risk than you would to purchase the 60-day call. Should the stock suffer a significant decline, then the loss will be greater than the original 62.5 cents that you wished to invest. It is not sufficient to assume that you will exit the trade when you have lost this 62.5 cents, because you may have to sacrifice some of the time that the 60-day call afforded you. Overall, it can be said that you should plan to choose and hold options that have a 70- to 110-day life span in order to maximize your chances. To sum up the above criteria:

- The option should have close to 90 days before expiry.
- The option should be trading near- or at-the-money.
- The value of the option should double if your forecast is correct.
- Your forecast should require no more than a 10 per cent advance in the stock within the specified time.

What to do next

Having decided to make such a calculated investment as buying a call option, you should back your judgment by holding it until your forecast price has been reached. This does not preclude purchasing a longer-dated option to hold for a shorter time specified by that forecast. It simply means that you should not change your tactics unless your forecast on the underlying security has changed. But keep this thought in mind. If you are managing your money properly, your forecast should not change simply because you feel "the pinch," or you can't afford the loss. Your forecast will, I hope, be based upon sound fundamental reasons.

There are three cases when you should consider subsequent action now that you own a call option:

1. The stock has declined and so has your option. In this case you must assume that you are running out of time and your prediction for the stock is not unfolding as you had hoped. Otherwise, you should continue to hold the call and not second-guess yourself. It is worth mentioning here that you should never average down. This is the practice of purchasing more of the same security as the price lowers, thereby reducing your average cost price. Averaging down completely distorts your system of money management and will rarely fulfill the initial purchase criteria mentioned above. It is not possible to average down with options in the pure sense of the term as you would with stock. Although you may be able to purchase more of the same series of calls that have declined in price, they will not have the same time left until expiry that your original calls had when you purchased them. Your original calls may have had 90 days to expiry but by the time that you average down they may have significantly less time remaining. A more common alternative in the options market is to roll down.

Rolling down is the practice of selling the existing calls you hold and purchasing calls with a lower strike price. For instance, let's assume you purchased the 90-day call with a strike of $25, but the price of the underlying stock declines to $23.50. Your call is now almost worthless and the prospect of the stock returning to a level of profitability is looking bleak. Rolling down would require that you sell your $25 call and purchase the $22.50 call instead. You are in effect chasing the stock on its way down in the hope that it will eventually rebound and you will recover your loss. This practice is not recommended. It is a way of pyramiding your losses and defeats one of the natural advantages you originally enjoyed as a call purchaser: that of limited risk. Rolling down is a recommended strategy for buyers and sellers of puts, and will be discussed shortly. The best course of action when facing a loss on a call purchase is to clearly reassess the investment. Don't invoke emotions that cause you to feel that the market owes you, or that you can't be wrong. The market does not owe you anything, and, yes, you can be wrong.

2. The stock has stayed the same and your option has declined. In this case rolling out is an often-used tactic. Rolling out involves the simultaneous sale of the option you hold and the purchase of another call with a later expiry month. It is used to extend the time of the investment and the chances of eventually realizing a profit. This tactic should only be considered as a second investment decision and not as a continuation of the first. It is not sufficient, or recommended, to assume that you will eventually be right. The only thing that this line of thinking will accomplish is the depletion of your capital. Remember, part of your forecast included a time frame as well as a price movement. By rolling out, you are changing your forecast of the time frame in which the price movement will occur. If it didn't happen as you planned then it is better to take the disciplined approach and admit that your forecast was wrong. You should only resort to rolling out your call options if you have made a second clear investment decision, one that also requires 10 per cent of your risk capital. But do some soul-searching and ask yourself honestly if you are not just chasing your original investment, rather than making a new and calculated one.

3. The stock has advanced and you have a useful profit. In this event, you will be in the happy position of having capitalized on your investment and doubling your money before the expiry of your call option. You now have several choices beginning with simply selling the call. When asked how he had become so wealthy, Baron Rothschild once replied, "I sold too soon." I mention this to emphasize that there is no shame in taking the profits you have made. There is also nothing wrong with researching a stock, making an investment and realizing a profit according to your forecast. In fact, it is quite exhilarating. However, you will never get rich if you continue to quit in the middle of your winning streaks — unless your name is Baron Rothschild. The advice from most of the more successful money managers is consistent: Keep your winners and sell your losers. In the case of a profit with a call purchase, there are several ways to cash in some of the paper profit while maintaining a position that will continue to profit from further price advances.

The following are some of the possible actions you might take in the event that you have achieved an appropriate paper profit on your call:

Roll up. You have already seen that your calls can be rolled down or out, but they can also be rolled up. This involves selling the existing call and purchasing a call with a higher exercise price. Let us suppose that we had purchased the 90-day calls with the strike price of $25 for a cost of 87.5 cents a call. Subsequently, the stock advanced from $25 to $27 within a 45-day period. Your calls also advance from 87.5 cents to $2.375. You have more than doubled your original investment and are now tempted to exit the trade. You don't want to lose the gains already made, however, and you also believe the stock may continue to move up in price. A possible tactic in this position might be to roll the calls up to an exercise price of $27.50. A 45-day call with a strike price of $27.50

might be trading at approximately 50 cents. You would be able to sell your original calls for $2.375 and purchase the $27.50 calls for 50 cents, for a credit of $1.875. Now you would still own the same number of call options and continue to profit from any further price advances, but you would also have cashed in a very good profit from the original investment. The original calls were purchased at 87.5 cents and you were able to roll them up for a credit of $1.875, making your profit, so far, $1.125. You would have more than doubled your money and still owned a position from which to profit. There is also nothing wrong with simply selling out the position and taking a profit of 11/2 points. Indeed, the most attractive part of this strategy is the selling of the original calls, taking your profit and reducing your risk. But occasionally lightning does strike, and the stock may continue to climb to even greater heights. This strategy will allow you to benefit when it does just that.

Roll out. Rolling out a winning position is not really a consideration for some of the reasons described earlier in this chapter. It is a method of extending the time frame of an investment. In this case, you are seeking to maintain a bullish position to profit from continued price advances. The problem is that it normally requires an additional investment. You will now have more funds at stake than you originally did, and you still won't have captured any of your paper profit. Trust me, there is nothing worse than having realized a profit on a well-researched stock only to see it disappear because you changed your mind and became more aggressive in the middle of the strategy. Rolling out is not recommended because it does not allow you to take any of your funds out of the market. It also involves an additional investment which distorts your money management scheme. Unlike rolling up, it is an additional investment and should be made as a separate decision.

Create a bull spread. Creating a bull spread is another tactic that, like rolling up, allows you to cash in on some of the existing profits while maintaining an exposure to the underlying stock. Instead of selling your existing call, you create a spread by selling a call with a higher strike price. Suppose in the above example where your stock advanced to $27, the $27.50 calls were for some reason trading at or near 87.5 cents, your original cost price. It would then be possible to sell the $27.50 calls and recoup your original investment. You would also have an opportunity to profit if the stock continued upward, but you would have limited your profit to 2 1/2 points with the spread.

Given a choice between creating a bull spread and rolling up, I much prefer the latter. A bull spread is too limiting to your profit potential. Assuming you are bullish on the underlying stock, the returns do not seem to justify the risks of the stock declining and resulting in the loss of your paper profit. While this and other spreads have their usefulness as strategies, it does not suit the purpose here where you seek to capitalize on existing profits. Using spreads is only recommended as a complete strategy and not as an adjunct to an existing call or put position. You may find situations that are more attractive than the example I have used here. For instance, a spread where the differential is five points rather than 2 1/2 would be a good starting point. But for my money, I would rather do nothing.

Do nothing. Enjoy the ride. Brag to your friends. Get rich. Just don't let that profit slip away. Assume this is one of the four times in 10 that you will have a winner. Don't lose it. Don't quit the position in the middle of the winning streak. If the going starts to look a little rough, either consider rolling the call up and taking some of the profit, or sell the position entirely.

To sum up, I rank your possible actions in the following order:
- Do nothing.
- Roll up if you can take a profit which doubles your money.
- Create a bull spread.

I cannot recommend rolling out. I am firmly of the mind that you should always seek to preserve your original profit. Thus, if you choose to do nothing and hope for a continued advance, you should also watch the position closely and mentally place a stop-loss order, or an exit point, at a price that will still assure you of a profit that doubles your original investment. This will allow you to maintain your position during a winning streak. If the stock corrects to the price level of your mental stop-loss, take the disciplined approach and exit the trade.

Buying puts

Unlike buying calls, buying puts is a bearish strategy. You buy puts when you expect that a particular security will decline. The strategy of buying a put option has many similarities to that of buying a call. Like the holder of a call, the holder of a put has the right to choose

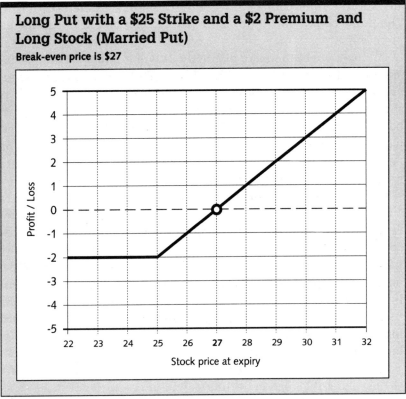

Long Put with a $25 Strike and a $2 Premium and Long Stock (Married Put)

Break-even price is $27

CHART VIII

when to exercise his option. Both strategies are sensitive to time and direction. Because the life of an option is limited, time is always working against the option purchaser. Whether it be puts or calls, the value of the option is constantly eroding as time ticks away toward expiry. If the underlying stock does not experience a price move, then the option will lose its premium and you will suffer a loss. As with calls, the put buyer risks losing his entire investment.

There are generally two ways of profiting from a market decline: Sell the stock short; or purchase a put option. The greatest advantage of purchasing a put option is that the loss is limited to the premium paid. This is a direct contrast to selling stock short where the potential loss is unknown and unlimited. Furthermore, the put buyer does not have to be responsible for any dividends the stock may pay, or run the risk of being bought in if their broker is unable to borrow the stock; though the short stock seller is not restricted by any specific time period in which to capitalize on his investment. The profit potential of a put is limited to the stock price minus the premium.

Oddly enough, there are distinctly different rather than opposite uses to puts as opposed to calls. This is perhaps because most investors tend to purchase securities rather than sell them short. A short sale is considered hedged with a long call, while a long position is considered insured with a long put. The connotations of an insured position are proper investment and risk management while hedgers are associated with arbitrage. The truth is that both are equally valid investment positions.

Both types of investors use options in legitimate situations to transfer risk away from their portfolio, even if their investment forecasts are at opposite ends of the spectrum. It is my view that a true speculator is someone who does not transfer any of the risk away from his investment. He remains exposed to the vagaries of the market by maintaining a wide-open, or unhedged position. He has little regard for money management and lacks discipline. The speculator seeks the maximum possible return and has little regard for the risk he assumes. Typically, speculators are also great users of leverage.

One of the common uses of puts is to insure a stock or portfolio against a possible market decline — without requiring that the stock or portfolio be liquidated. The same can be said of calls but only when you have a short stock position or a large diversified short stock portfolio. The short portfolio type is quite rare in comparison to the long stock portfolio. Thus calls are not associated with insurance in the same way as are puts.

Chart VIII represents the purchase of stock at $25 and the simultaneous purchase of a put with a strike price of $25, for $2. The strategy of purchasing a stock and simultaneously purchasing a put option is known as a married put. Note that this graph is exactly the same as the graph for a long call. You can achieve the same position by simply purchasing a call. There are technical differences such as dividends and interest on the cost to carry the stock, but the profit/loss outcome is the same. The cost of the put increases the break-even point of the stock, but it limits the loss of the entire investment to the exercise price of the put less the amount of the premium, as does the purchase of a call. This is known as put-call parity.

It is defined by the equation:

Long T-bill + long call = long stock and long put

Both positions have identical profit and loss distributions. It is also another example of how at-the-money puts will always have a slightly lower price than the corresponding calls. Both positions have theoretical unlimited profit and risk the loss of the premium paid for the option. If both options were priced the same, you would always purchase the call and the T-bill because of the cost to carry the stock. Market-makers use this knowledge to purchase the call and the T-bill, and sell the stock and the put. Said another way, this is an illustration of how puts and calls are really the same thing.

Using puts and calls with a stock position

From time to time you will have made a somewhat speculative purchase of a stock and it will have performed well over time. On these rare occasions, you would be in much the same position as you were with the profitable call positions mentioned earlier. Many of the choices of subsequent action are relatively the same as with calls although, in this case, you are the owner of stock and not an option. You can now use options to fine-tune the stock position. There are basically five things you could do with our winning stock position.

1. Sell the stock and replace it with a call. This is a good alternative to consider when you believe the stock may continue its advance but you are concerned about losing the profit you have already achieved. Perhaps you purchased the shares on speculation that some event, such as a lawsuit, may go in favour of the company. The shares have advanced but the outcome of the lawsuit is still uncertain. There is still room for advance if the company wins the lawsuit but you would like to be certain of the profit you have on paper. In this case, you might consider selling the stock to realize the profit, and purchasing a small amount of call options to maintain an exposure to the stock. The attractiveness of this strategy is your profit is now in the bank, and you can still profit from continued advances in the share price. The disadvantage is that you may not realize as much profit as you normally would have because of the money spent on the calls. If you choose this tactic, I recommend only a small portion of the profit be spent on the replacement position to ensure that you enjoy as much profit as possible from the stock position.

2. Sell a call to create a covered write position. While it is impossible to create a true bull spread as with the case of a profitable call position, it is still possible to sell a call. You will in effect be creating a covered write position by being long the stock and short a call. The advantages are basically the same as with any covered write position, you receive additional funds that are direct profit and you have some downside protection. The disadvantages are also similar: You limit the upside potential of your stock position, and you remain exposed to a correction in the shares. Covered writing will be discussed in detail in Chapter 9. Personally, having had the happy experience of choosing a winner in the market, I would prefer not to use this strategy because if I was willing to continue to hold the stock I would not want to limit my profitability. Nor would I wish to see the stock decline and lose the good profit already achieved with only a small call premium to show for it.

3. Buy a put for insurance. Buying insurance with a put option is a possibility that will lock in your profit for the cost of the premium on the put, but only for a limited period of time. This strategy is very similar to replacing the stock with a call since you have assured yourself a profit on the stock and have an opportunity to profit from continued advances in the stock, but pay a small amount of your profit to do so. This is a strategy I have never used, partially because it is so rare that I pick a winner good enough to have the problem of choosing subsequent action. But, conceptually, it is a contradiction to me that I am holding stock while worrying about a price decline. I would prefer the leverage afforded by replacing the stock with a call position rather than reducing my future profit immediately with the purchase of a put. Note that with any small future advance in the stock a call position will continue to profit while the put purchaser will not, until the incremental advance on the stock has paid for the cost of the put premium. Given the situation and the choice, rather than purchase a put I would sell the stock.

4. Sell the stock. You picked a winner and have a profit. A very wise floor trader once told me, "You will never get hurt by taking a profit." This is good practical advice. Don't get fancy now that you have a little knowledge of option trading. "Buy low, sell high" is still the winningest of strategies in the stock market and you have the chance to use it here. Don't give back any portion of your hard-fought profit.

5. Do nothing. Like the profitable call owner, you may sit back and enjoy the ride. Experts continue to advise that you should keep your winners and sell your losers. You can always re-evaluate whether the stock should be held at current levels. There is no need to feel that you should give back a portion of your profit by putting on an option position unless the option will deal with the uncertainty in an appropriate manner.

To recap, I rank your alternatives this way:

- Do nothing or sell the stock. These two are ranked equally because they simply involve your own analysis of whether the stock is a good investment or not. After all, you have done well. Why lose confidence in your ability to evaluate it now?
- Sell the stock and replace it with a call. This choice is ranked second because it affords the best opportunity to continue to profit through the use of leverage, limits your risk because you no longer have to hold the stock, and ensures that you exit the original trade as a winner.
- Buy a put for insurance. This still allows you to profit if the stock continues to advance, but it is ranked lower because the decision to use this strategy assumes some uncertainty regarding whether you should hold the stock at all.
- Sell a call and create a covered write. This alternative is not recommended. It limits your profit and leaves you exposed on the downside in return for a small premium. Covered call writing is a neutral strategy that makes the most sense when a stock is not expected to move significantly one way or the other. If this is the case, you should exit the trade.

Exercising your options

When you exercise a put or call option, you are initiating a trade in the underlying stock. In effect, you are buying or selling a stock at a predetermined price. Your broker will charge you a commission for this service just as he would for any stock trade. There are basically only two situations where you should ever consider exercising a call or a put option. The first is obvious. You definitely want to purchase or sell the underlying stock. I am not concerned with why you want to own a security. If you want to own the stock outright, by all means exercise your option.

The same goes for selling the stock. You may have planned to dispose of a certain stock if the price declined to a certain point, and had purchased a put option as insurance to do so. You may wish to remain exposed to the price movement of a stock and request that your option be exercised. In this case, the result will be a short stock position. You will of course now assume all of the risks of being a short seller. But if you have good reasons for selling the stock short, I'm not going to tell you not to do it.

The second and real reason for exercising an option is that it may be more profitable for you to do so than to simply sell the option in the secondary market on an exchange. From time to time, options that are very deep-in-the-money will trade at a discount to their intrinsic value. For instance, when Popular Gold Stock trades at $43, the bid for a PGS August 30 call option may only be $12.50, even though it has an intrinsic value of $13. This occurs when interest in that series of option has dwindled due to the lack of leverage it offers, or the limited time remaining to expiry. If someone were to buy this call then he would ultimately have to exercise it and sell the stock to realize his profit. Since such transactions cost money, market-makers will not pay you full value for the option. They will typically buy the option at a small discount to pay for their costs to perform the stock transaction at expiry. You must decide whether it is cheaper for you to sell the option at a discount or to pay your broker the commissions to exercise the option, buy the stock and subsequently sell it. The cost of trading the stock may be more than the discount you give up to the market-maker. It is important to remember that if you have sold an option and it is trading at a discount to its intrinsic value, you are extremely likely to be assigned the underlying stock.

CHAPTER 7

Strategies for Selling Calls

THE STRATEGIES OF SELLING uncovered calls and puts have been placed in separate chapters because of the importance of understanding them conceptually and their advanced nature. Uncovered, or naked, writing means that the position is not hedged or covered in any way by some security, and the seller has the pure risk of the difference between the exercise price of the option and the price of the underlying security at expiry. A long put or call may also not be hedged or covered by some other stock position, but unlike a short call or put, the risk is always known. The only factor which will mitigate this theoretical loss is the premium received for selling the option. In the case of a call, it can be covered simply by owning an equal amount of the underlying stock. But this is not so with a put. There is no underlying equivalent which will satisfy the obligation to purchase a stock at a certain price except cash. Thus the only way to be purely covered if you sell a put is to possess an amount of cash equal to the exercise price of the option. In essence this does not really mean that you are covered, it only means that you will be able to absorb the maximum possible loss which may result.

Oddly enough, the risk profile of selling a put is considerably different than that of selling a call. Harrison Roth points out in his book *LEAPS* that it is unfair and even offensive to place both of these strategies in the same category. Selling calls has an unlimited risk, as does the strategy of selling stock short. Selling puts has a limited risk, as does the simple strategy of purchasing a stock. In fact, most investors are completely unfamiliar with selling stock short. But almost every investor has at some point in their life purchased a stock. Selling a put is actually less risky than purchasing a stock, because the loss resulting from a price decline is offset by the premium received for selling the put. It is the naked and unlimited risk associated with selling call options that is responsible for the image options have of being risky and speculative investments. Mr. Roth simply states that he does not recommend this strategy under any circumstances. I am sympathetic to this view because it is rarely necessary to sell naked calls to profit from a bearish-neutral outlook on a particular stock. In fact, it is probably the only option strategy that I have never employed.

On paper it is easy to see that the profit/loss picture of selling options is simply the opposite from that of purchasing them. In practice, you have given up the right to act and are therefore obligated to another investor. This means that you might be called upon to fulfill your obligation at an inconvenient and expensive time. It may be inconvenient because it can happen at any time during the life of the option and you have no control over when it may occur. Selling uncovered options is also a strategy that requires strict discipline and well-defined objectives. The punishment is swift and sure for the undisciplined option seller.

There are many things to understand about being in such a position where unlimited loss is possible. For instance, an experienced trader told me recently that whenever you sell uncovered options you can expect that at some time during the life of the strategy you will be in a losing position. When I considered this, I realized that it was true of the naked option positions I had written. Like many, after I wrote an option I assumed that it would merely be a matter of sitting back and waiting for time to pass and reduce the value of the option. I quickly learned that this was rarely the case. Unless you pick the top or bottom price for the underlying stock when you write an option, it will usually experience an adverse price move. It is important to be aware of this possibility so that panic does not set in when it happens. This is why I emphasize the importance of maintaining a disciplined approach to the strategy. Define your objectives clearly and choose a price for the underlying stock at which you will say to yourself, "I was wrong and should buy back the option to control my losses." After you write the option, it would be ideal for it to decline over time gradually and eventually expire unexercised. Unfortunately, it is just not possible without a great deal of luck to pick the bottoms or tops of stock prices. Be sure to stick to your forecast when you write uncovered options and expect that at some point during the life of the option you may be in a losing position.

I recently wrote some at-the-money puts on a stock trading at $45. Shortly thereafter, the stock rose to well over $50 and I was ruing the fact that I hadn't just bought the stock or bought calls instead. I was even contemplating rolling the puts up to a strike price of $50 in order to capture some more premium. Was my original forecast wrong? You bet. The stock proceeded to fall all the way to $38. I was suddenly looking at a significant loss on my options. I was also now congratulating myself for not buying the stock or calls, and instead choosing the more conservative strategy of writing puts. The truth is that I might have closed out the puts when they were in a winning position and over half of their value had eroded. Then I might have been able to truly congratulate myself on making a winning trade. The moral of the story is that there are many learning experiences awaiting you in the market. Particularly when you are employing a strategy such as naked writing. Understanding aspects of trading such as this, and maintaining a disciplined approach will keep you in good stead in the long run.

A curious aspect of market-makers is their goal not to be in such a position. Many retail investors subscribe to the misconception that the only way to make money with options is to sell them. They wrongly assume that market-makers have a huge advantage just by virtue of being able to sell puts and calls at the most favourable market price. For the most part, market-makers do not wish to be exposed to the direction of the market. If, as a market-maker, you are constantly short options, whether puts or calls, at some point in your career disaster will strike. It could be a takeover bid while you are short calls, or some sort of crash while you are short puts. But eventually you will suffer some enormous loss which could put you out of business. Market-makers have no desire to risk being knocked out of the game over one position and they take great care to avoid directional risk.

If you don't think disaster can strike, I would like to relate one last anecdote. Recently, a friend and I were discussing the market in general, and the many stocks that had fallen from great heights and were now trading for pennies. We made a list of eight stocks and contemplated buying some nominal amount of each in the hope that one or two stocks would recover and return to their former levels. We named it the "poor man's basket" because of the small amount of capital required to purchase this group of securities. Each of these eight stocks had at one time traded for at least $14 and some for as high as $38. Though we never did execute the strategy, I mention it to illustrate the unpredictability of the stock market. No one in a million years would have predicted that these stocks would have fallen so drastically. But imagine the losses that took place when they did. And imagine the devastation that resulted to those who had written naked put options on these stocks. The point is that you must be prepared for the worst extreme when you sell uncovered options. The strategy of naked writing should never be used for speculation.

Selling calls

Selling calls is a neutral to bearish strategy. You can use it to profit from a sideways or bearish stock market. If you think that a stock's price will remain level or decline, you can sell calls. Selling a call obligates you to sell the underlying stock at a predetermined price, the strike price, to the holder of the option upon his request. While the risk associated with a short call is theoretically unlimited, this is only true during the life of the option. As a strategy, selling calls is less risky than selling a stock short.

Chart IX illustrates the profitability of a short call option where the premium is $2, and the exercise price of the call is $25. The break-even point is reached when the stock trades at $27 because the obligation to sell the stock at $25 is offset by the $2 premium received for selling the call. The maximum profit is achieved when the stock is at or below the exercise price of the call and never exceeds $2. Beyond the break-even price of $27, the position begins to lose money dollar for dollar until infinity. But remember, the risk of a short call is limited by its life span. Furthermore, there may be considerable margin for error as any loss is reduced by the premium received for the call. In Chart IX, if your forecast of the stock is wrong you will not begin to lose money until the stock price exceeds the strike price plus the premium received.

The potential profit of short stock is considerably greater than the potential profit for a naked call. Compare Chart X to Chart IX. The naked call writer's profit is limited to the premium while the short seller will continue to profit until the stock reaches zero. In return for this, the short seller assumes the theoretical risk of the stock rising to infinity. Of course, you can also achieve greater profitability by writing calls that are deeper in the money and have larger premiums. But the further in-the-money the call, the greater the risk. In

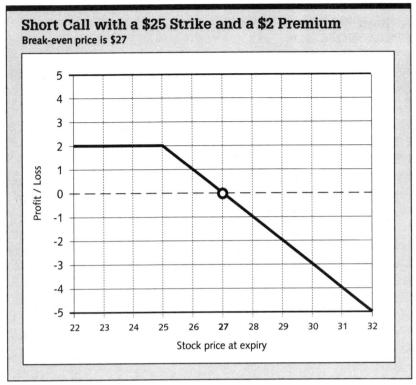

Short Call with a $25 Strike and a $2 Premium
Break-even price is $27

CHART IX

fact, you can almost achieve a similar position to a short sale by writing very deep-in-the-money calls.

In Chapter 4, we discussed how it could be advantageous to purchase a 90-day option and hold it for a period of only 60 days. This tactic avoids losing a large part of the time value in the final month of expiry. Conversely, when you sell a call or put, the opposite is often the best strategy. The value of an option declines most rapidly during the final days prior to expiry. The most profit is also realized from a short option during this time. If you sell a longer-term option, the price decline will be somewhat slower in the early days of the option unless the underlying security experiences a favourable price movement. But you do not anticipate that this will be the case or you would not have used the strategy of selling a put or a call, you would have simply bought a put or call. The strategy of selling options is intended to capitalize on a neutral period in a stock's life. The best way to do this is to capture the time frame where the op-

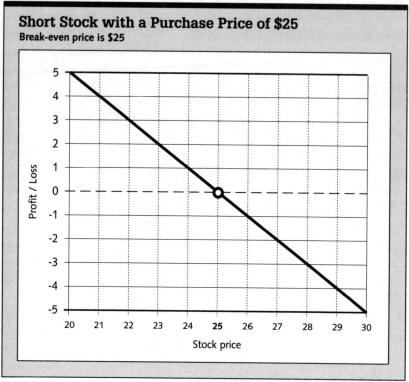

Short Stock with a Purchase Price of $25
Break-even price is $25

CHART X

tion is losing its time value the fastest. This is in the final month or so of an option's life. If you were to sell an option in the early days of its life you would wait some time for this value-erosion to occur. You should sell an option with a shorter life span than the one you would look to purchase.

What to do next
The only real case where you must contemplate action with a naked call position is when the underlying stock has increased in price. You should not be too concerned in the event the stock remains neutral or declines since this was effectively your forecast when you wrote the call and you have a profit. No action is required while the call is declining in value. But when the stock has advanced beyond your exercise price you run the risk of being assigned. There are three choices to contemplate assuming that you do not want to accept the assignment and sell the underlying stock.

1. Buy the option in the market. The alternative is the most basic. You have executed a simple naked write, and it has not performed as expected. You should close it out and accept your loss. This is the best approach when you are not engaged in some type of systematic writing program. If it was simply an individual investment then it is usually best to accept your loss and buy back the option. It is also the disciplined approach. Indeed, the real disciplined approach would be to place a target price for the underlying stock where you will buy back the call to avoid a large loss. You may also be buying back the option to realize a small profit. If you had written a call with a strike price of $25 for a $2 premium, you might be able to buy back the option at a cost of $1 and realize a $1 profit.

2. Roll the option out. Rolling out a long call position was a method of extending the time of the position at a greater cost than your original investment. The reverse is true when you have sold an uncovered option. It is also one of the advantages of having time on your side. Assuming that you are content to continue to hold a short call position in the underlying stock, then a possible choice is to repurchase the call and sell another one with more time remaining on it. This can usually be done at an additional credit to the one already received. For instance, assume you have sold a call with an exercise price of $25 for a $2 credit, but as the expiry date approaches you are disappointed to see that the stock has rallied and the call is now worth $3. However, you note that a longer-dated call is worth $4. In this case, you could repurchase the call you wrote for a $3 premium and sell the longer-dated call for $4, netting a further $1 credit. You have now maintained your original exposure to the stock and increased the credits you received for writing the call. The downside is the additional time remaining for the call to expire. Ultimately, you run the risk of the stock continuing to advance in price and chasing it up forever — or until you are out of funds.

There are many possible variations of this strategy. One is to sell a greater number of the new calls to pay for the repurchase of the original ones. This in effect pyramids your exposure to the underlying stock and can lead to enormous losses if you do not have the capital to renew the position each time it approaches expiry. But with patience, it can eventually pay off. Unless you are a sophisticated investor who fully understands the risks of rolling out, and have significant capital at your disposal, I do not recommend entering into a naked writing strategy with the intention of continuously rolling the position out.

3. Roll the option up and out. This is somewhat more conservative than rolling out. It involves buying back the calls you have written and selling more calls with a later expiry date, but also with a higher strike price. This gives the position less probability for disaster as the stock must again move against you for a loss to occur. The downside is that, again, you continue to be exposed to the stock. You also do not receive as large a credit for selling the call with the higher strike price. In fact, you may not be able to execute this transaction at a credit at all unless you sell a greater number of the new calls, thereby increasing your risk.

Assuming you are the type of investor who is sophisticated enough to engage in this type of activity, then the best choice for subsequent action is rolling out. This also assumes that you have entered into the strategy with a long-term systematic approach and intend to continuously roll the calls out. If one of the features of selling options is that time is on your side, then you should take advantage of it. As long as you continue to receive credits for selling the calls all is well. Selling calls does not require a cash outlay, only margin, so that any credit received is additional income to your portfolio. The average investor does not have the resources or sophistication to enter into this type of call-writing strategy. If you must write a naked call, then research the underlying stock carefully, establish clear objectives of when to close out the position, and be disciplined enough to stick to those objectives. Even a seemingly conservative approach to naked call writing, such as writing far out-of-the-money options, which also has a high probability of achieving a small profit, can result in financial ruin if some event such as a takeover in the market occurs.

Aggressive rolling
There is another way to manage your naked writing program which is also the most aggressive. I call it aggressive rolling. To be sure, it is only for the most sophisticated trader who also has significant amounts of capital in reserve to support the strategy. It involves continual rolling of the options that have been sold to the strike price closest to the stock. It begins with the simple sale of some amount of options which should not require more than 5 to 10 per cent of your capital to margin with your broker.

Let's assume the stock is trading at $45 and you sell some puts with a strike price of $45. If the stock rises to, say, $50, the strategy would call for you to buy back the 45 puts and sell some puts with a strike price of $50. Depending on the time elapsed, the new puts that are sold will likely have a longer time to expiry than the original puts. If the stock were to decline from $45 to $40, the same thing would be done. Buy back the 45 puts and sell a later-dated put with a strike price of $40. If the price of the stock were to stay the same, then the puts would be allowed to expire. The intention is to continue to take in credits with each option that is either sold, or rolled in to. Over time not only are many credits captured but the option seller also takes in the maximum credit from continually being short the at-the-money options. You can see that, especially in the case of call writing, this strategy can require enormous resources and can also lead to significant and devastating losses.

Consider the case of a stock that begins to steadily advance. A call seller must continue to repurchase the calls at a loss and resell another option. As the price advances, more and more options must be repurchased and sold. The price may begin to advance so rapidly that further credits are not available and many transaction costs must occur. Eventually, a large portion of capital will be lost and the investor may have to simply exit the strategy with his resources severely reduced. In the past couple of years, there have been examples where this strategy would have been absolutely clobbered if certain stocks had been chosen. One technology stock experienced a meteoric rise from less than $5 to over $180. Another U.S. drug company rose from below $20 to $147. Not stocks that you would have enjoyed writing naked calls against. But over time, this strategy will eventually profit even with some adverse and severe market moves, if you have the capital and nerves to support it.

You can see that the strategy of writing naked calls is only for the most experienced and well-capitalized investors. Even professionals are reluctant to employ naked call writing and do not wish to hold such positions for long periods of time. It is not only the risk of financial disaster, but also the fact that if it occurs, you will be out of the game and have no chance to recover. And don't discount the personal and emotional hardship that can follow from financial ruin.

CHAPTER 8

Strategies for Selling Puts

WHENEVER YOU SELL A PUT option you are acting like an insurance company. In return for a premium, you agree to purchase an underlying security at a predetermined price, for a stated amount of time. You assume the risk that the security may suffer a drastic decline, and you might have to purchase it for an amount substantially greater than the prevailing market price. A friend of mine who was once a market-maker has a favourite expression, "Never sell puts unless you are long puts." The fact that he was formerly a market-maker might give you some hint as to why he has a particular disdain for this strategy. If you guessed that he suffered tremendous losses from large naked put positions which wiped out his capital you would be right. I do not happen to share his negative opinion of put writing because I believe the real culprit in his experience was the word large.

Any time you extend yourself and take on positions which may be beyond your financial means, you set yourself up for a disaster. Remember, it is not just the strategy you employ that defines your risk, but also the size of the investment, whether you are diversified, and whether you can afford a potential loss. I emphasize that special care must be taken when selling puts or disaster may indeed result. Used carefully, put writing can be more conservative than even purchasing a stock. Used carelessly, or for leverage, and put writing can result in financial ruin.

Selling puts

Selling puts is a neutral to bullish strategy. You can use it when your forecast for a stock, or the market in general, is flat or bullish. Selling a put minimizes your risk by giving you downside protection. You will still incur a loss if the stock suffers a decline, but your loss will be reduced by the premium you received. However, the premium also limits your potential for profit.

Chart V illustrates the profit and loss potential of a short put. The premium for the option is $2, the strike price is $25, and the break-even price is $23. The maximum profit can never exceed the premium received for the put, $2. The loss begins with an amount equal to the exercise price minus the premium and continues until the underlying stock reaches a price of zero.

This profit and loss potential is identical to another well-known strategy, covered writing. Both strategies share similar characteristics. I believe that covered writing, discussed in detail in Chapter 9, is a far more popular strategy because investors lack proper understanding of both strategies. Most brokerage houses require that you have more capital to sell puts than they do for simple covered writing. This prevents some clients from being able to use a put selling strategy.

Selling puts versus placing an open buy order
From time to time you may want to buy a stock at a certain price. Let's say it currently trades at $25. You are willing to buy the stock at some lower level so you call your broker and enter an open buy order for the shares at $24. This instructs your broker to purchase the shares at $24 or better for some stipulated period of time. If the price declines to that level he will try to purchase the stock for you. If it stays above that level, your order will not be filled and you will still have your cash. Selling a put option is a useful alternative to entering an open buy order. I must emphasize that it is a good alternative only if you are willing to own the stock at $24 in the first place. With the stock trading at $25, you might choose to sell a put with a strike price of $25, for a premium of $1. The results at the expiry of the option are shown in Table VIII.

You can see that selling a put is a far better alternative than waiting for the stock to decline to a price where you might be willing to purchase it. The key here is not to put the cart before the horse. You must decide that you are willing to buy the stock at some predetermined price level before you contemplate selling the put. Do not begin a put writing program without knowing that you want to own the stock at that price. That way, if the stock falls below $24, then you won't be disappointed or any worse off when you suffer a loss. In all the other profitable cases the strategy will be working for you. Besides, this is also a much more active strategy than doing nothing and waiting to have an open buy order executed. You will be

The Profit Potential for Selling a Put Option versus Entering an Open Buy Order

Stock price at expiry	Profit
greater than $25	$1
$25	$1
between $24 and $25	$1 minus the difference between $25 and the stock price
$24	same as stock purchased from open buy order
less than $24	same as stock purchased from open buy order

TABLE VIII

adding the premium you receive for the put, and interest on the premium, to the return you are already getting on your cash portfolio. You will see in the next chapter when we discuss covered writing that if you are assigned the shares after writing the put, that further downside protection can be obtained by selling covered calls.

There is a small disadvantage to selling a put compared to placing an open buy order. An open buy order can easily be cancelled if you change your opinion of the stock. But as a put seller, you would have to repurchase the option and might suffer a loss by doing so. In practice, the loss should be relatively small except in the case where trading in the stock is halted and the stock opens much lower. When a stock is halted, the trading of its options is also halted. This prevents you from taking any defensive action, while the open buy order could simply be cancelled. Despite this, I feel that the advantages of selling puts far outweigh the possibility of this type of event occurring.

Selling puts to reduce your cost base for acquiring stock is another conservative approach to writing puts. This is because the puts that are sold are necessarily out-of-the-money. The likelihood of being assigned the shares is considerably less than if you had written an at-the-money or in-the-money put. This strategy can be made even more conservative by selling further out-of-the-money puts. If in the above example you chose to sell a put with a strike price of $24, then the stock would have to fall below $24 minus the premium received for the put before you would be in a loss position.

Of course, the return on your investment would be reduced because the premium for the put with the lower strike price would be somewhat less than for the put with the exercise price of $25. It is a risk and reward calculation that you should make based upon your evaluation of the underlying stock and your ability to assume risk. The aggressiveness of the strategy is defined by the strike price of the put. If you choose to write an in-the-money put, then the risk of loss is considerably higher, as is the probability of loss. Remember that the further the option is in-the-money, the less time premium it will have. This reduces the attractiveness of selling the put in the first place. Selling in-the-money puts should only be done if you are definitely willing to purchase the stock. I don't believe that this makes very much sense because of the lower percentage return caused by the fact that if the stock remains stable then the put will have to be repurchased. A further disadvantage is that you still have a limited upside potential. If the stock should experience a dramatic advance, you will not be able to profit beyond the amount of premium you received for the put. I think it's better to buy the stock if you are willing to take the risks associated with selling the in-the-money put.

Selling an at-the-money put is a way to achieve the maximum possible gain from a neutral to bullish outlook on a stock. Remember that at-the-money options have the greatest amount of time value. This is what I term a slightly aggressive strategy because of the losses that can result from a rapid decline in the stock price. Again, I must emphasize the importance of doing your homework on the investment quality of the underlying stock. If you are unwilling to own it then do not write puts. Compared to a straight purchase of stock, selling at-the-money puts is somewhat more conservative because of the downside protection afforded by the premium received. But this fact alone should not make you rush out and sell puts. You should consider that it is a better alternative to buying the stock. This may be the case if you feel that the stock is not likely to experience a rapid advance or decline in the near future.

What to do next

Assuming you have sold puts as recommended and not for speculation, then there will be very little need for subsequent action. If the stock does not decline, the option will simply expire and you will have realized a profit. You can then re-evaluate the stock to determine if you should again sell puts, purchase the stock, or do nothing. If the stock declines below your strike price of $25, you will probably follow through on your original strategy and take the stock when it is assigned to you at $25. However, if you sold the put with the intention of buying the stock if it declines by expiry, only to see it slightly lower than when you sold the put, you have realized a profit. In this case, there are three actions you may choose from:

1. Do nothing. You will be assigned to buy the shares at the exercise price of the put. You are ahead of the game a bit because your cost base for the shares is less than they are trading for in the market. Your objective has been achieved. You have purchased the stock for a net cost of the amount you were originally going to place the open buy order for, and the stock is already trading higher. Be sure to notice if there might be a dividend due on the stock soon after the expiry. This might make assignment more attractive.

2. Repurchase the put option. You sold the option for $1 and can now buy it back for somewhat less. It is probably a good idea to re-examine whether you still want to own the stock. Has anything changed your original outlook on the stock? If your outlook has changed, then repurchasing the put is a good alternative. Simply buy the put back, pocket your profit and move on to other things.

3. Roll the option out (or down and out). Rolling the put option out is reasonably attractive in this case. You buy back the put you sold, and sell another one with a longer expiry date. You may want to be more cautious by selling a put with a lower exercise price, rolling down and out. Yes, you can be more aggressive also by choosing a put with a higher exercise price, rolling up and out, but this is not recommended for reasons stated above. Rather than roll the puts up, I prefer to accept the assignment and buy the stock. By rolling the put out you capture another premium. This will reduce the cost base of any eventual purchase of the shares even further.

The only great disadvantage to choosing this action instead of buying the stock is the upside potential of the stock. Remember that when you roll the put out you are maintaining an exposure to the stock. You should ensure that your view of the underlying stock hasn't changed for the worse. If it has, then repurchasing the put option is by far the best choice. Also bear in mind that the probability of incurring a loss increases the longer you are exposed. Just because your strategy is successful does not ensure that it will continue to be. Having made these warnings, I prefer rolling the option out. This is largely because you continue to take in credits on a stock which you feel is of investment quality, but you are not allowed to make a capital outlay. Note that if you had bought the stock originally you would have had a small loss. Selling puts has brought a profit, and the ability to roll out further reduces the loss and even the possibility of a loss.

Don't overextend yourself

Many investors feel that they can sell a great many out-of-the-money puts because of the conservative nature of the strategy. Selling puts can lead to significant losses in a bear market even if you employ it in the most conservative manner. Who hasn't seen a stock suffer a drastic decline as the result of some unforeseen event? I have seen many investors sell far out-of-the-money puts with very little time to expiry, and receive a premium as small as 6.25 cents for doing so. One investor in particular did this for quite a long period of time. That is until one day, just prior to expiry, the stock plummeted by over $17. This investor suddenly had losses of over $35,000 (U.S.). You need only look to the 1987 crash to see what can happen to speculators who sell more puts than their resources can bear. As I have recommended this strategy for investors who may be contemplating the purchase of a stock at some level below its current market price, I must emphasize that the number of puts you sell should never exceed the amount of stock you are willing to own. The temptation to do this is greater than you think. You should always consider what the result would be if the stock falls dramatically and prepare yourself for that outcome. You probably would not mortgage your house to buy a stock, so why assume the risk that you might have to do just that if the stock falls.

CHAPTER 9

Covered Writing Strategies

COVERED WRITING INVOLVES
the simultaneous purchase of a stock and sale of a call option on
that stock. If you were to sell a call without owning the underlying
stock you would be exposed to theoretically unlimited losses. The
stock may be the subject of a takeover bid and should the price advance rapidly you would be exposed to serious losses. The way to
collect the premium for selling the call option without exposing
yourself to this type of risk is to purchase the stock to cover the call.
The call is considered covered because the investor can deliver the
stock if the holder of the call exercises his option. In return for
agreeing to deliver the stated amount of stock, at a stated price, for a
stated period of time, the covered writer receives a premium. This
premium greatly enhances the yield or benefit of owning a stock. It
also provides the investor with some immediate income and, to a
degree, reduces the cost of owning the stock, and provides him with
some downside protection. The risks associated with covered writing are the same as those associated with owning stock. But these
risks are reduced by the premium received for selling the call option.

Like selling puts, covered writing is a neutral to bullish strategy.
Chart XI shows the profit and loss picture of a covered write. The
stock is trading at $25 and the premium of the call is $2. The profit
is limited to the amount of the premium received. The break-even
point is reduced by $2. And the potential loss is the same as it is for
stock ownership minus the $2 received. The profit and loss picture
would change slightly depending on the exercise price of the call
option and the amount of the premium. You can choose to be more
aggressive with this strategy by selling a further out-of-the-money
call. Or you can be more conservative by selling a further in-the-
money call. Readers who are catching on to these profit graphs may

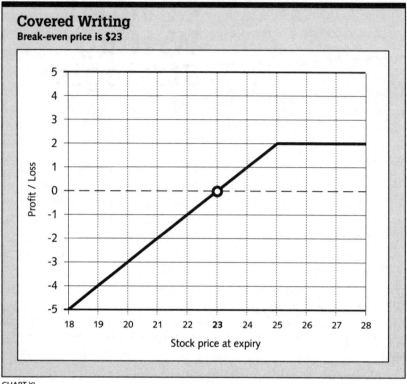

Covered Writing
Break-even price is $23

CHART XI

have noticed that this graph is identical to one we have already seen, Chart V the short put graph.

The identical profit and loss picture is created if, instead of the covered write of a call with a strike price of $25 for a premium of $2, you sell a put with a strike of $25 for a premium of $2. When you write the put you can avoid the cost of carrying the stock and reinvest the excess funds in a T-bill. However, unlike the stockholder and covered writer you won't receive any dividends. This is partly the reason why puts always trade at a slightly lower premium than calls with the same exercise price and expiry date. If the premiums were the same, it would be a simple matter for the marketmaker to sell the stock short, buy a call to protect the short position and simultaneously sell a put to pay for the call. Thus any risk-free opportunities such as this quickly disappear. The buying pressure for the calls, coupled with the selling pressure on the puts, creates a slight difference in prices, even though the underlying stock may be trading at exactly the exercise price.

A popular strategy

Next to purchasing puts and calls, covered writing is by far the most popular option strategy. There are several reasons for its appeal. Covered writing is conceptually easy to understand, and it is a simple trade to execute. It involves owning stock, something most investors have had some experience with. Covered writing provides immediate income while owning the stock, and it increases the investment yield of the stock. Finally, it provides additional protection in the event of a decline in the price of the stock.

This is a pretty impressive list of advantages. In fact, it is hard to imagine a better strategy if all this is true. But there are some disadvantages to covered writing. You assume the risk of owning the underlying stock. You forfeit your profit if the stock advances. And you might forfeit additional income if the stock is called away prior to paying a dividend

The first risk cited here is something most investors readily dismiss since they are usually willing to be owners of the stock. But you should definitely not enter into a covered writing strategy unless you want to own the stock. Don't let some of the apparent yields of a covered writing strategy seduce you into purchasing the underlying stock. Do your homework before buying any stock, whether you intend to write calls against it or not.

The biggest criticism of this strategy is that it eliminates winners from your portfolio. You can enhance the yield on a stock by a couple of percentage points, but by committing to deliver the stock at the exercise price, you forfeit any profits over and above that price. Let's face it, sometimes lightning does strike. Your stock might soar. When it does, however, you will be relegated to watching from the sidelines while other investors revel in their good fortune. On the other hand, if that same stock were to fall drastically, you would be forced to endure the brunt of that loss. The only mitigating factor would be that small amount of premium that you received in exchange for holding the stock. This scenario underlines the importance of your forecast for the underlying interest of the options you are trading.

No one emphasizes this as well as my colleague Alexander Gluskin in his excellent book *Confessions of an Options Strategist.*

There is simply no substitute for doing your homework on the underlying stock. One of the most common mistakes made by the covered writer is to look for a high return by buying a stock and selling a call. This puts the cart before the horse. You should not buy any stock unless you have first done your research and deemed the stock to be of investment quality. Once you have done this, you can further analyze the investment to see if it fits in with a covered writing program.

Another major mistake made by covered writers is to sell calls against stock they hold in order to obtain some downside protection. You shouldn't be concerned with downside protection when considering this strategy. If you truly suspect that a stock you hold will suffer a price decline, you should sell the stock, or buy a put as insurance.

Using a covered writing strategy

This example, excluding commissions, shows how using a covered writing strategy enhances the yield of a long stock position. It is based on the actual bid/ask prices of a listed stock, but I will continue to call it Popular Gold Stock.

Buy 100 shares Popular Gold Stock @ $33.375 $3,337.50
Sell 1 PGS August 35 call @ 1.60   160.00
Break even   Cost of the stock minus the call premium

If, by August, Popular Gold Stock trades at or below $35, the call will not be exercised. You will still own the stock at a net cost of $3,177.50. In this case, the standstill yield of this strategy is 19.18 per cent (a three-month call). Of course, any standstill return is a good one by definition, since others who simply owned the stock earned nothing. The covered writer is able to add the premium of the call to any dividend received for an enhanced yield.

But if, by August, Popular Gold Stock trades above $35, then the call will be exercised and the stock sold at $35. In this case, the maximum yield of the strategy is achieved. It makes no difference whether the stock trades at $35.125 or $100, the profit here remains the same: the premium received ($160) plus the sale price ($3,500) minus the purchase price ($3,337.50), or $322.50, a 38.65 per cent return.

A loss occurs when the stock declines below the break-even point of $3,177.50. However, at the expiry of the first call option you have written, a second one may now be written. In effect, this starts the strategy all over again. This will further reduce the break-even price of the stock. In fact, this strategy can continue to be re-peated until you have secured a profit. But the stock cannot con-tinue to fall. If it does, you should re-evaluate the investment quality of the stock.

The yield and break-even price of a security can be adjusted by selling a call with a different exercise price. The bias of covered writing remains neutral because of the opportunity to profit when markets are moving sideways. During bull markets, it would be bet-ter to own the stock outright, or buy a call. During bear markets, it would be better to sell the stock.

Covered writing can be tailored to an aggressive or a conservative investment strategy. This is done according to the amount of pre-mium you receive for selling the call. The more premium received, the more conservative the strategy. The higher premium affords the maximum downside protection. In order to achieve this higher pre-mium, it is necessary to sell a call option with a lower strike price. But the lower strike price will limit your profitability in the event of a price advance.

If you want to be more aggressive, or you forecast a price advance in the stock, you can sell an option with a strike price that is higher than the trading price of the shares. How aggressive you wish to be will determine how much higher. But while allowing some room for the stock to advance, you give up the higher premium of a call with a lower exercise price and the protection it affords.

Systemic writing

Systemic writing is a way of using covered writing over and over again. In its purest form, it begins with you writing a put option, being assigned and purchasing the underlying shares and sub-sequently writing calls (and even more puts) on the newly acquired shares. The purpose of this strategy is to continually take in premi-ums from writing several options on the same security. It will nor-mally be successful over a period of time unless the stock suffers a rapid decline. I will discuss systemic writing in more depth in the advanced strategy chapter, but I mention it here because you can enter into a covered writing program with the intention of continu-ously writing calls after each one expires. If you have written a Popular Gold Stock August 40 call, two things may occur at the third week of August when the call is about to expire. It will be in-the-money. Or it will be about to expire worthless. If the latter is the case, then there is little to worry about. On the following Monday, you can write another call to continue the strategy and gain more income. If it is in-the-money, then there are other things to consider. Do you allow your stock to be called and be content with your profit? Or do you want to keep your stock and continue the writing program? These are decisions that you need to prepare for in advance. If you want to continue the writing program, it may be a simple matter to repurchase the calls you wrote, and write calls with a longer expiry date. This is known as rolling out. The calls that are about to expire will have very little premium left and will normally be trading for much less than the call with a longer expiry date. Any decision you make will depend upon whether you want to continue to hold the stock and the amount of premium you will receive for the longer-dated call you sell.

Using systemic writing

Here is a possible scenario for the Popular Gold Stock shares in the previous example. Let's assume the shares are trading at $42 when the August 40 calls you wrote are about to expire. The August 40 calls are priced at $2.125. The PGS November call prices are:

November 35	$7.125-$7.25
November 40	$3.00-$3.25
November 45	$1.50-$1.75
November 50	$0.25-$0.50

This example leaves you with four possible courses of action. You can roll out, roll up and out, roll down and out, or do nothing.

1. Roll out. If you roll out, you must repurchase the August 40 call and sell a November 40 call. This can be done at a net credit of $3 minus the $2.125 required to repurchase the August call, or 87.5 cents. While this is not a significant gain in terms of premium, the downside of holding the stock will not be a worry until the stock dips below the exercise price of $40. You are committed to sell at $40 so you won't care how high above the exercise price it is in November. Twenty-five cents or $18 will mean the same to your profit picture. When you roll out you usually expect the stock to remain neutral. If you want to continue the covered writing program on this stock then this type of trade will allow you to avoid the transaction costs of being assigned, selling the stock and subsequently repurchasing it to write more calls.

2. Roll up and out. To roll up and out, you would repurchase the August 40 at $2.125 and sell the November 45 call for $1.50. While this would involve a cost to you of 62.5 cents, it would raise the price at which you must sell the shares to $45. This gains you the profit of $2 which is represented by the current price of the call. However, it would drastically reduce the downside protection that your current position affords.

3. Roll down and out. To roll down and out is not really viable here since the time value of the November 35 call is only 12.5 cents. There is no real point to this strategy as it only postpones assignment and being forced to sell the stock. At the same time, it prolongs the holding period on the stock and carrying costs for no apparent purpose.

4. Do nothing. Allow the systemic writing strategy to come to an end. Accept your profit and look ahead to your next investment.

Your choice of action will depend largely on how aggressive you wish to be and whether your view of the underlying security has changed or not. All are good possibilities here with the exception of rolling down and out. Personally I am inclined to do nothing and accept my gain. When the trade was made there was a possibility that the stock would advance beyond $40 but I would still profit. Thus, if I wished to continue some similar writing program on the stock I would simply sell a put with an exercise price of $40 and avoid both the cost of repurchasing the call and carrying the stock. Note that in the future if the stock declined below $40 I would be faced with much the same choices as listed above.

CHAPTER 10

Strategies for Spreads

YOU CREATE A SPREAD WHEN you buy and sell different options of the same type (either puts or calls) that normally share the same underlying interest. The long option in the spread does not expire before the short option does. Spreads are generally described as vertical, horizontal or diagonal. This stems from the way in which option quotes first appeared in the financial press. Each series of option was listed vertically by price. A price spread came to be known as a vertical spread. The different months of each option series were listed across the page horizontally. For this reason, calendar spreads are also known as horizontal spreads. A diagonal spread combines both time and price. It is possible to create a spread between different underlying interests. A spread involving a treasury bond future and a Euro-dollar future is known as a TED spread. But such spreads are beyond the scope of this book. The spreads in this chapter have only one underlying interest. They also have a clear-cut market bias. Most of the spreads encountered here can be easily executed. You might well consider using one of them at some point or another. More advanced spreads, used by market-makers and professionals, are covered in a later chapter dealing with advanced strategies.

Spreads usually involve the creation of a window of profitability, or loss, between the exercise prices of two puts or calls, or between two different times in the future. A spread is always created using either a price or a time difference, and it will often encompass both of these characteristics. The execution of a spread is usually accomplished as a simultaneous trade. However, it is possible to execute one side of the transaction first, and execute the other side of the spread sometime in the future. This practice is known as "legging" because you buy or sell one leg of the spread at a time. Legging into or out of spreads is often used as a manner of adjusting an existing position, such as a long call or put, in order to enhance its profitability or to provide some protection. It is not advisable to attempt to leg into or out of a spread simply as a method of improving the price of the eventual position. You immediately assume the risk that the price of the second option may move against you, and dramatically, before you can enter the second part of the spread. This type of trading is characteristic of indecision and speculation since it implies that you are unsure of the trade you want to execute or the price you are willing to pay. If you decide against executing the second part of the spread because of an adverse price movement, the position now has become a plain long position. This was not your original, and it has already become a losing position. Be sure about your strategy and the price at which you are willing to have it executed. Otherwise, you have eliminated one of the greatest advantages of using options, that of knowing and limiting your maximum loss.

Commissions and margin

Commissions and margin are important considerations for the spread trader. Previously, experts advised small investors against the use of spreads because the transaction costs were exorbitant. You had to pay one commission for the buy side and an additional commission for the sell side to open the position. Then you had to pay two commissions again when the spread was closed out. Four commissions for one trade. There is even a facetious name for this strategy. It's called an alligator spread because commissions eat up all of your capital. Times have changed, however, and brokers have adjusted their commissions to account for the option spread trader. In addition, discount brokers now provide experienced investors the opportunity to make trades at further reduced commissions.

Margin is good faith money that an investor lodges with his broker when he enters into certain trades. Your broker is not in the business of accepting the market risks of your trades any more than he is in the business of sharing in the profits of them. He will request that you post an amount of margin sufficient to the difference between the exercise prices of the particular spread. This amount also represents the maximum risk the investor is assuming for the transaction.

Bull call price spread

The dynamics of a price spread involve selling one option and simultaneously purchasing another. Spreads have a wide appeal to the investor who wants to sell options to capture the premium, but doesn't want to assume the risks of the uncovered option writer. Here is an example of a bull call price spread:

Buy 1 PGS August 25 call	$3
Sell 1 PGS August 30 call	$1
Net debit	$2

By purchasing an August 25 call, you have the right to buy the stock at $25 until August. At the same time, you are obligated to sell the stock at $30 for the same time period. If you are assigned your obligation to sell the stock at $30, then you can exercise your right to purchase the stock at $25, guaranteeing a $5 profit. As a buyer of a spread, your market bias is bullish. You will profit as the underlying stock moves above $25. But the sale of the August 30 call limits the profit of the spread once the underlying stock reaches $30. The August 25 call will cost more than the August 30 call. Your maximum profit from this spread is the difference between the exercise prices ($5) minus the initial net cost.

Chart XII illustrates the profit graph of a bull call spread. The August 25 call was purchased at $3 and the August 30 call was sold for $1. This makes the net cost of the spread $2. The maximum loss is the net cost of the spread, and the maximum profit is the difference between the exercise prices minus the cost of the spread. This spread appeals to the investor who is basically bullish on a stock but is not optimistic enough to think that it will advance more than $5 in a given period of time. To this degree, the spread trader is somewhat akin to the covered writer in their willingness to forfeit larger gains for a more conservative return. Another characteristic of this type of option strategy is selling one or more options to pay for the initial transaction. While this is usually characteristic of a spread, there are other situations where it is possible to do this, such as ratio writing. By selling the August 30 call in our example, you reduce the amount of your investment in the August 25 call.

A spread transaction is normally placed with your broker as a single order with a net debit or net credit, to ensure that both sides of the trade will be executed at once. It is possible, of course, to purchase one side and later sell the other side of a spread, or vice versa. The major disadvantage or risk to the spread trader is the possibility

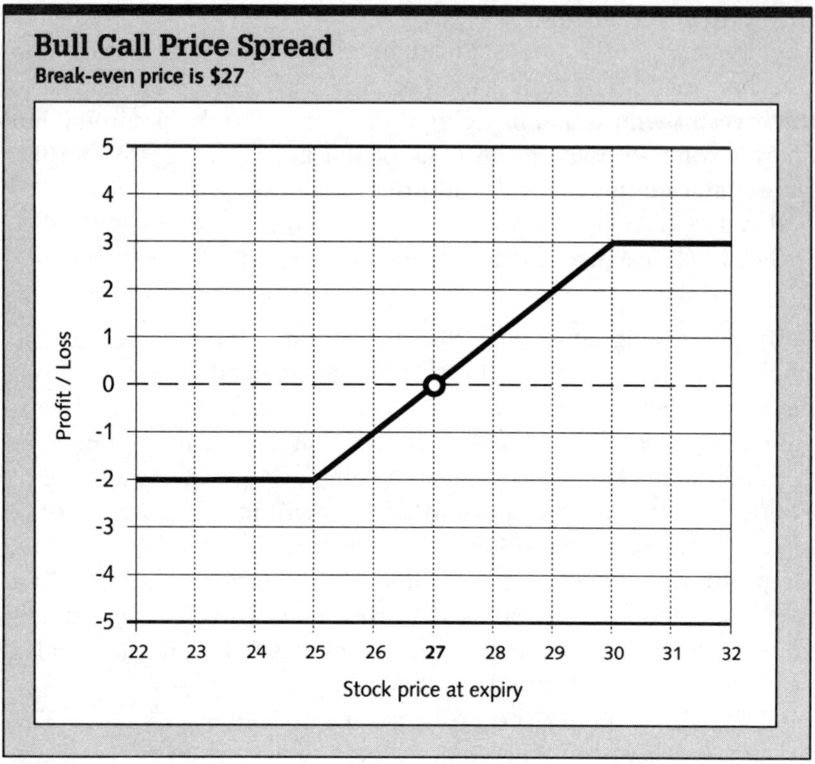

Bull Call Price Spread
Break-even price is $27

CHART XII

of early assignment. The holder of the short option that has been sold as part of the spread may, during its lifetime, wish to exercise it to receive the underlying stock. This may occur when the stock is due to pay a dividend, for instance, and the investor may not be able to exercise the long side of the spread in time to receive the stock and offset that dividend. Any investor who has a spread position should pay close attention to the ex-dividend and expiry dates.

Bull put price spread

You can also create a bullish spread using puts instead of calls. The major difference, other than the type of options used, is the exercise prices bought and sold in the spread. An example:

Buy 1 PGS August 25 put	$1
Sell 1 PGS August 30 put	$3
Net credit	$2

Now the relationship between the prices changes. The option being sold has a greater value than the one being purchased. This changes the profit and loss graph slightly. Now the maximum profit is the total credit received for writing the spread, or $2. The maximum loss has increased to the difference between the strike prices minus the premium received for the spread, or $3. The option purchased is completely paid for, and more, by the one which is sold. This is also known as a credit spread because the investor actually receives a credit when the trade is executed. The market bias of the spread is still bullish because it will become more profitable as the stock advances. This is largely because the higher-priced option has more to lose than the lower one. In a credit spread, the purpose is not so much to pay for one option with the sale of another, but to cover or limit the loss on the sale of an option by purchasing another. Generally speaking, when you buy a spread it will become more profitable as the prices between the options widen. When you sell or take in a credit for writing a spread, it will become more profitable as the prices between the options narrow.

Bear call price spread

It is a simple matter to reverse these strategies by buying the August 30 calls and selling the August 25 calls. This creates a bear call price spread. Instead of paying a $2 net cost for the spread, you receive a net credit of $2. The bear call spread involves selling the option with the higher exercise price and buying an option with a lower one. The object is to profit from the sale of the call without assuming the risk of a sharp increase in the price of the stock. You limit this risk by buying another call, one with a much lower exercise price. You pocket the premium, earn interest on it, and sit back and wait for the options to expire — hoping that the stock will not advance beyond $25.

There are several variations of this spread depending on how aggressive you want to be. You can be more aggressive by selling a deeper-in-the-money call, for which you will normally receive a larger credit. The question of how much risk to assume is one that can only be answered by comparing your objectives with the profit and loss potential of a particular strategy. An unlimited loss strategy is not suitable for someone with a fixed income who seeks preservation of capital. If you are unsure of the suitability of a strategy to your particular investment need, then you should almost certainly consult with a professional.

Bear put price spread

A bear put price spread involves the simultaneous purchase of a put and sale of another put with a lower exercise price. Here's an example:

Sell 1 PGS August 25 put	$1
Buy 1 PGS August 30 put	$3
Net debit	$2

Again, this strategy seeks to partially pay for the purchase of the August 30 put with the sale of the August 25 put. In this case, you are bearish, but you don't anticipate the stock falling below $25. The sale of the August 25 put limits the potential profit of the purchase of the August 30 put, but it is in turn protected or covered from its maximum loss by the purchase of the August 30 put.

Calendar or time spreads

A calendar or time spread is more sophisticated than a price spread. It involves the simultaneous purchase and sale of two options of the same type, with the same underlying security, but with different expiration months. For this reason, it is also known as a horizontal spread. The exercise prices may differ depending upon how aggressive, bullish or bearish the investor chooses to be. The calendar spread is designed to profit from the erosion of the near-term option occurring at a faster pace than the longer-term option. To this extent it is a neutral strategy, although it can be tailored to become more bullish or bearish. In our discussion of the time decay curve we saw how the value of an option erodes more quickly as it approaches expiry. Table IX illustrates how a calendar spread is expected to profit over time.

Using this table, let's create the simplest example of a calendar spread. When the stock is trading at $25, you choose to sell the 30-day call with a strike of $25, and purchase the 60-day call with the same strike price, at a net debit of 12.5 cents. Assuming the stock remains at $25 until the expiry of the 30-day call, you would expect the 60-day call (which still has 30 days left to expiry) to have a value of 75 cents, or the value of the previous 30-day call. Your original investment, or debit, of 12.5 cents is now worth 75 cents, a 62.5 cents profit. The profit has resulted from the fact that the original 30-day call has expired worthless, and the 60-day call has retained most of its original value. You can see that this strategy would not work if the value of both options eroded in a straight line. If that were the case, then the most you could hope for would be to break even.

You could also amend this strategy to make it more bullish by selling the 30-day call with a strike of $27.50 and purchasing the 60-day call with the same strike. You have now in effect created a diagonal spread. If the stock remains unchanged at the expiry of the 30-day call, then we would expect the original 60-day call to still have a value of 12.5 cents. The transaction would look like this:

Sell 30-day call strike of $27.50	12.5 cents
Buy 60-day call strike of $27.50	31.25 cents
Net debit	18.75 cents

If the stock remains unchanged in 30 days, the 30-day call would expire worthless and the 60-day call would be worth 0.125. The end result would be a loss of the original net debit (18.75 cents) minus the value of the remaining call (12.5 cents), or 6.25 cents. You would not use this strategy if your outlook on the underlying stock were neutral. However, if you were slightly bullish over time and expected the stock to rise to the $27.50 level then the profit picture would change dramatically. At the expiration of the 30-day call, if the stock had risen to $27.50, you would expect the original 60-day call to have a value of 62.5 cents, or the original value of an at-the-money 30-day call. Then you would have a profit of the remaining call (62.5 cents) minus the original debit paid for the spread (18.75 cents), or 43.75 cents. You would have more than doubled your money, because the spread would have widened from 18.75 cents to 62.5 cents.

The astute reader will have noticed here that you would have made a tremendous profit by simply purchasing the 30-day call with a strike of $25 for 75 cents, if at expiry the underlying stock were to advance to $27.50. You can see here that this strategy is not best used when you are purely bullish on a stock. Although one of the advantages of a calendar spread is that the loss is limited to the original debit, a calendar spread rarely loses all of its value. This is because the remaining option will usually have a value at expiry. But the major use of a calendar spread is as a timing tool. It can be used to capitalize on anticipated events which are expected to

The Profit Potential of a Calendar Spread with 30-, 60- and 90-Day Call Options

Stock Price = $25

Strike price	30-day term	60-day term	90-day term
$20.00	$5.125	$5.375	$5.500
$22.50	$2.625	$3.625	$4.375
$25.00	$0.750	$0.875	$1.250
$27.50	$0.125	$0.3125	$0.500
$30.00	$0.0625	$0.125	$0.250

TABLE IX

occur within a certain time frame. It can also be used to spread the risk of certain option positions over more than one expiry period.

With virtually every option investment, there are two factors which must be fulfilled for a profit to occur: direction and time. In a calendar spread there can sometimes be a third aspect to the investment: "not too much direction." In other words, in the case of the bullish calendar spread, you would like the stock to advance to approximately $27.50, but not too far beyond. Once the stock advances beyond $27.50, both options will begin to lose their leverage and the spread will actually begin to narrow again. The maximum gain for a calendar spread is when the stock is trading at the strike price of the expiring option. Thus the criteria of the stock performing as expected over time also becomes more narrowly defined. You hope that the stock moves up in the first 30 days but only to a certain point. Notice that in a price spread it did not matter how much the stock advanced or declined. Once your maximum profit or loss occurred it could not change no matter how much further the stock continued beyond our exercise price. For the retail investor, I would recommend this strategy only if some or more of the following conditions apply:

- The short-term option will in all likelihood expire worthless.
- The near-term options are overpriced, and there is no good alternative call to purchase, or put to sell.
- If an advance in the stock is anticipated it is expected to occur slowly so that the near-term option will not benefit.
- A dramatic increase in the underlying stock is not anticipated.
- There has been an increase in volatility, making the near-term options more expensive than usual.

There is another way to execute this strategy, which in effect is a type of surrogate for covered writing. You can sell the near-term call and purchase the longest-term call. The idea behind this tactic is that you expect the near-term call to expire worthless. When it does, you intend to write the next near-month call, effectively creating another calendar spread. I call this a surrogate covered writing strategy because the long-dated call replaces the need to actually own the stock to cover the short-term call. Let's look at another example using Table IX. First you:

Sell 30-day call, $25 strike	75 cents
Buy 90-day call, $25 strike	$1.25
Net debit	50 cents

Assuming the 30-day option has expired worthless as expected, you then:

Sell next 30-day call, strike of $25	75 cents

If this call expires worthless as well, you will have taken in two premiums of 75 cents each and paid out a premium of $1.25, for a net credit of 25 cents. And you will still be able to sell the remaining 30 day call for 75 cents. The total return for these transactions, less commissions, will be:

Buy 90 call	$1.25
Sell 30 call	75 cents
Sell 30 call	75 cents
Sell 30 call	75 cents
Net profit	$1

Needless to say, the underlying stock will have to cooperate for all of this to come true. But I have been slightly unfair in my example because most investors who employ this calendar writing system will have written near-term out-of-the-money calls, increasing the likelihood of them expiring worthless. The strategy will be examined more closely in the chapter dealing with long-dated options known as LEAPS. It is important to note that in any calendar spread, if both options are in-the-money at expiration then the spread will have to be closed out. This involves the expense of two more commissions. Furthermore, if the near-term option is assigned prior to expiration and you are forced to sell the stock prematurely, you will usually have to buy back the stock and sell the long-term option to close the entire position. The commissions on these transactions will eat up the profit you may have made on the spread.

And they could easily cause a loss. In short, there are many things that will have to happen for this strategy to work for the most investors.

CHAPTER 11

Advanced Option Strategies

THE ADVANCED STRATEGIES in this chapter are nothing more than combinations of the strategies discussed earlier in this book. You can significantly alter the risk and reward profile of a basic strategy simply by buying or selling an additional put or call. Many of the advanced strategies also combine one or more basic spreads. As you will see, changing the expiry date of any option in a strategy will radically change the profit potential of a strategy. But with every additional position you add to a strategy, you need to employ a commensurate amount of skill, care and thought to make your strategy successful.

Straddles

You create a straddle by simultaneously buying or selling both a call and a put of the same underlying interest. The call and put must share the same exercise price and the same expiry date. A straddle is an extremely bearish or bullish strategy. You use a straddle to profit from a dramatic price change in the underlying security when the direction of change is uncertain. For example, let's say you know that the outcome of a major lawsuit will make or break a company, but you can't predict the court's decision. You could use a straddle to profit from such a situation.

A strategy that will realize a profit no matter in what direction the stock moves appeals to many investors. However, if the stock remains neutral, your profit is eliminated. Because buying a straddle involves owning both a call and a put, a price move in the underlying stock is essential if the position is to profit. When you purchase a call or a put, time works against you. The value of an option erodes as the expiry date approaches. This effect is even more pronounced when you buy a straddle because the value of both options declines with the passing of time. You must be sure that a

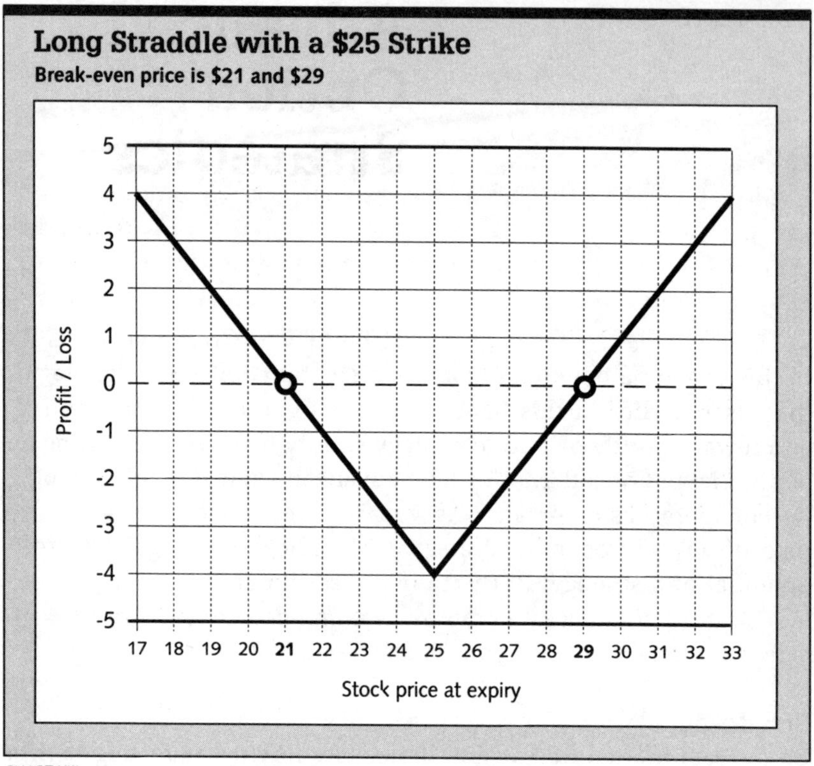

Long Straddle with a $25 Strike
Break-even price is $21 and $29

CHART XIII

directional move in the stock's price is imminent before employing this strategy.

The profit and loss graph of a long straddle looks like Chart XIII. The graph illustrates the profitability of purchasing a straddle with a strike price of $25. There are two premiums, $2 for the put and $2 for the call. The maximum loss of the strategy occurs when the stock trades at exactly $25 at expiry. In that case, neither option has any intrinsic value. A straddle has two break-even points because it involves two options. In Chart XIII, they are $21 and $29. Because the total premium is $4, you need the stock to move at least $4 in order to break even. You can see that the probability of a loss is quite high since a very large price movement in the stock will have to occur in a short period of time. Conversely, the probability of the maximum loss occurring is quite low since this would require that the stock trades at exactly $25 when the options expire. But if the stock remains neutral, you lose your entire investment. The position could be quite profitable. The call could theoretically rise to an unlimited value, or the put could climb in price if the stock fell to zero.

In practice, straddles are rarely used in the marketplace. Lawsuits that make or break a company are comparatively rare. And rest assured that market-makers are usually aware of such pending events and will price their options accordingly. The puts and calls on that stock will be extremely expensive to purchase. In my experience, most investors prefer to choose one possible outcome of a lawsuit, and then purchase a put or a call. The straddle purchaser is not predicting the direction of the stock but rather a large price swing. Because of this uncertainty, straddles have little practical value for the investor beyond that of speculation. There is little reason to get involved in some situation where a stock's fortune is unknown. If you insist on taking a chance on this type of stock, then you would be better off evaluating the event and making a calculated directional investment. You could even use a spread to minimize your losses in the event that you are wrong. If you decide to become a straddle purchaser, remember to choose options that expire somewhat after the date of the event expected to influence the stock price. That way if you are wrong and the stock price remains the same, there will still be some premium left on the options you purchased and you can avoid a total loss.

Combinations

A combination is similar to a straddle except that it involves the purchase of a put and a call with different strike prices. The expiry month of the options will usually be the same, although it doesn't have to be. Using the straddle example, a combination could involve the purchase of a put with a strike price of $22.50, and a call with a strike of $27.50. The combined cost of the two options would be somewhat less than the straddle with the strike $25, perhaps costing only $1. The area of maximum loss has increased dramatically, between $22.50 and $27.50, but the amount of that loss has decreased. The potential profitability is similar to the straddle since the call and put could rise dramatically. However, a maximum loss still occurs at $27.50, whereas with the straddle, only a small loss would occur since the call would have some intrinsic value at expiry.

Combinations are preferable to straddles for most investors because of the reduced capital expenditure and the potential for large gains if the stock experiences a large price swing. Their use is still somewhat limited because of the speculative nature of the strategy as well as the few opportunities where they can be applied. A combination is also sometimes called a strangle. Unlike a straddle, it can be used with both in-the-money and out-of-the money options. In the above example, you could instead purchase a $27.50 put and a $22.50 call, ensuring that wherever the stock price finishes at expiry, one of the options will have some intrinsic value. The cost of both premiums will always exceed the difference in the exercise prices (in this case, $5) so a significant move in the stock is still required or a loss will result. The move would have to be at least beyond either of the strike prices.

Short straddles

You create a short straddle by simultaneously selling both a put and a call of the same underlying security. This is not a strategy for the timid or those who have difficulty sleeping at night. A short straddle allows you to profit from a stable market environment, but you assume a high level of risk. Your profit is limited to the total amount of premium received. And because the position involves a naked call, the loss is theoretically unlimited. But the probability of loss is greater because the position is exposed in both directions. Any significant price move in either direction will result in large losses. Selling a put and a call on stock requires that you receive a large enough premium to reward you for the risk you are assuming. It also requires that you make a precise forecast about the direction of the underlying stock. That direction can only be neutral.

You will normally sell a straddle when you feel that the options may be overpriced. This doesn't just mean that the prices are higher than normal, but that the theoretical value of an option is implying that the volatility of the stock is unrealistic. Selling a straddle is recommended only to the most sophisticated investors who are able to accurately price options in relation to the expectations of the underlying stock. I have seen highly volatile stocks trading at $20 where a straddle consisting of a call and a put with strike prices of $20 had premiums totalling almost $10. If you purchased such a straddle, the underlying stock would have to advance beyond $30, or decline below $10 — a 50 per cent move — in order to realize a profit. The likelihood of such an event seems so remote that selling this straddle would seem to be a can't-lose proposition. What actually happened? Those who sold this straddle were quickly and severely punished when the price of the stock rose to $38.

There are few practical applications of this strategy for the average investor. It's not easy to outsmart the marketplace by guessing that option premiums will prove to be worth more than their intrinsic value at expiry, or that they are inefficiently priced. To bastardize a Latin phrase, let the seller beware.

Short combinations

Though less rewarding than a short straddle, a short combination is considerably less risky. This is because you can customize your strategy by choosing one of many different exercise prices. Typically, you would sell out-of-the-money puts and calls in combination. This reduces the probability of loss because the price of the underlying stock will have to move much further before a loss occurs. For this reason, a short combination is a more popular strategy than a short straddle. Using the example of the long combination, you can see that if you were to sell it instead of buying it, a very large price movement would be required for you to experience any significant loss. But as is the case with a short straddle, the most attractive options to sell are the ones with the largest premiums. Large premiums are the result of high volatility. Thus, you have a type of reverse Catch-22. The most attractive straddle and combination to sell are the ones with the highest premiums, but the options with the highest premiums will also mean that the underlying stock is the most volatile and carries the highest risk. A short straddle or combination writer has an extremely high vega risk. Vega is the anticipation of the amount of change in the price of an option for a one-percentage-point change in the assumption of the volatility of that security. It is discussed more fully in Appendix I. If the volatility of the underlying stock increases, then the premiums will also rise creating a losing position and greater risk. Margin calls may also result. In my years of observing option accounts I have never seen anyone consistently profit from this strategy without eventually suffering a heavy and devastating loss. If you decide on selling puts and calls simultaneously, do it selectively rather than systematically.

Covered straddles

To my mind, the term covered straddle is somewhat of a misnomer. This strategy involves the sale of both a put and a call when you own a sufficient quantity of the underlying stock to cover the call. A covered straddle combines a covered write with the sale of a put. However, the put is not covered as the name erroneously implies. The put also adds considerable risk should the stock price decline. Nevertheless, the covered straddle has proven to be the winningest or most profitable strategy employed by non-professional investors according to statistics compiled by the CBOE Options Institute.

If we alter the covered write example from Chapter 7, and add a naked put, we can create a covered straddle:

Buy 100 shares Popular Gold Stock at $3.375	$3,337.50
Sell one PGS August 35 call at $1.60	$160
Sell one PGS August 35 put at $2.25	$225

Now you own 100 shares of stock but are obliged to purchase an additional 100 shares at $35 if the holder of the put wants you to do so. In return for this obligation, you have received a premium of $225. The total premium received for the position is $385, or $160 plus $225. But you have also assumed the liability of having to buy 100 shares at $35 when they are selling in the market for $33.375. If the stock price remains unchanged, the return for each component of the strategy would be as follows: you would break even on the long stock, earn a profit of $160 on the short call and earn a profit of $62.50 on the short put. This scenario assumes that the put is closed out at parity – or at its intrinsic value.

The three-month yield on the covered write is 4.79 per cent, for an annual return of 19.18 per cent. The return for the covered straddle is 6.67 per cent, for an annual return of 26.67 per cent. (Dividends have not been added to the returns here.) The maximum profit is achieved when the stock trades at $35 or higher. In this case the profit on the stock will be $162. (Remember, the call you sold obliges you to sell the stock at $35). The profit on the call will be $160; the profit on the put will be $225. The total return here is a whopping 16.39 per cent, for an annual return of 65.6 per cent. If you merely owned the shares, the return would be 200 multiplied by $1.625, or $325, a 9.63 per cent return, or 38.5 annualized. By using options in a covered straddle strategy, the yield of the stock owner has almost doubled.

A covered straddle also reduces the downside risk of the position but only until a certain price level. After it reaches that level, the losses will escalate at a greater rate than with a simple covered write, because of the loss being sustained on the short put. The break-even price for the covered write is $3,177.50, or the cost of stock ($3,337.50) minus the premium of the call ($160). Note that at $3,177.50, the price of the put will be $322.50, or $3,500 minus $3,177.50. This also represents a loss of $97.50 (or $322.50 minus $225). The break-even point of the original covered write increases because of the sale of the put. The amount of the increase is equal to half of $97.50 because at $3,226.25 the loss on the stock is not as great. In other words, the break-even point occurs at a point where the profit on the call minus the loss on the put is equal to the loss on the stock. Where the original covered write would have shown a small profit, the covered straddle has shown a small loss. The breakven point for this covered straddle is composed of a loss of $11.25 on the stock, a profit of $160 on the call and a loss of $48.75 on the put.

Whenever you hear about tremendous annual yields like 65 per cent, you know there has to be a significant risk and this strategy is no exception. The downside to this strategy is that it gets absolutely clobbered in a bear market. You have double the exposure on the long side because of the short put. Remember that the premiums you receive will suddenly appear insignificant if the stock suffers a rapid decline. For instance, let us suppose the stock suffers a 10 per cent decline to $30.125. Now the total loss is $427.50, or 12.8 per cent, 51.24 per cent annualized. Note that with a 10 per cent decline the loss is greater than 10 per cent, because of the additional exposure created by the naked put. I must continue to stress that there is additional risk created by the naked put. The put is not covered in this strategy. There is no way of avoiding the exposure of the stock and the put. But there is a way of reducing risk to an acceptable level for your investment objectives while still employing this strategy.

Let's assume that you have done your homework and are ready to purchase 200 shares of some stock. Your forecast on the stock is that it is not likely to skyrocket immediately, or suffer a major decline. You decide that you can enhance your yield and receive some downside protection by employing a strategy of covered writing. Consequently, you decide to purchase 200 shares and write two calls. But you recall that you can further enhance your yield by writing two puts as well as two calls. Do not do this. You will have doubled your exposure to the downside with these short puts. By owning 200 shares as well as selling two puts, you will be potentially exposed to the losses of a 400-share position. This was not your original intention.

Instead, consider the following course of action. Buy only 100 shares, and write one call and one put. Now you will have assumed an exposure to the stock which you were originally willing to have when you decided to buy 200 shares. But you will have enhanced the yield of the position by the two premiums you have received as in the example above. If the stock declines, you will be in roughly the same position as you would have been had you purchased 200 shares and sold two calls. And you will be better off than had you simply purchased 200 shares without selling any options at all. If the stock advances, you will keep the premiums and any small increase the stock enjoys. Remember that a short put position has the same profit and loss graph as a covered write. Thus, you are really performing two covered writes with your covered straddle, one by actually buying the stock and selling a call, and one by selling a put.

Your subsequent action on this covered straddle position will depend on any reassessment of the stock you may have. You may decide to accept assignment of the stock for the short put if it is in-the-money and subsequently write more calls on the new stock. Or you may decide to close out the put or roll it out to another expiry and/or exercise price. If the stock advances and the call is in-the-money, you may wish to do the same with the short call. Buy it back and write another one with a later expiry, or simply let someone call your stock, and let the put expire. When I use this strategy, I know in advance what action I will take depending upon where the stock finishes at expiry. Rolling the put out and selling another call is my normal tactic when the put is expiring slightly in-the-money. I generally allow the call to be exercised if it is deep-in-the-money, and close the position. If the put is deep-in-the-money because the stock has declined, then I will usually close the position and accept my loss. You can tailor this strategy to suit your risk objectives. The more risk-averse you are, the further out-of-the-money the put you write should be. In the above example, you could have used a put with an exercise price of $30 instead of $35, and received a lower premium. This would reduce your risk considerably.

Butterfly spreads

A butterfly spread is also somewhat misnamed because it is really a combination of two spreads. The long butterfly spread is sometimes also called a sandwich spread. Many of the more advanced spreads we are going to discuss in the rest of this chapter are combinations of spreads we have covered in previous chapters. A butterfly spread combines a bull price spread and a bear price spread, but uses only three strike prices. A butterfly spread can be executed using either puts or calls. The market bias of a butterfly spread is neutral.
The mechanics of the butterfly spread are as follows:

Buy one PGS 22.50 call
Sell two PGS 25 calls
Buy one PGS 27.50 call

Chart XIV is the profit and loss graph of a butterfly spread. You can see that there are two spreads here: the bull spread of the long (22.50 call/short 25 call); and the bear spread of the short (25 call/long 27.50 call). You may also see where the spread gets its name; because of the wings created by the profit graph. The difference here is that you attempt to execute the position in its entirety at once. The premiums received from the sale of the two $25 calls (or in between calls) will offset the cost of the two long calls. The spread will reach its maximum intrinsic value when the underlying stock trades at the midpoint of the position ($25 in this example). If this trade could be executed for a net credit, an arbitrage opportunity would exist. The position is risk-free and the owner of the spread would have a profit. The spread becomes worthless if the underlying stock trades at the lowest strike price. It ceases to gain in value once the midpoint strike price is reached, because the short call negates the profits of the lowest long call. Your risk is limited to the debit paid. Finally, there is another small advantage to the position because of its neutrality. If the underlying stock does not change, the time decay of the two short options, which are typically at-the-money, is generally more rapid than the decay of the out-of-the-money. This is largely due to the fact that the premiums of the at-the-money options are higher so the price decline is steeper.

The non-professional trader will rarely have an opportunity to execute a butterfly spread for a zero or greater credit. In fact, even if

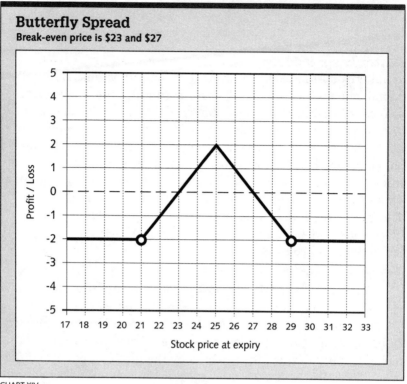

Butterfly Spread
Break-even price is $23 and $27

CHART XIV

the opportunity occurred, the commissions would likely eliminate any of the benefits. But because of the potential arbitrage opportunities for market-makers, the spread has important implications for the pricing relationships between options. The sum of the two midpoint calls must never exceed the sum of the lower and higher strike calls. Whenever it does, the market-maker will execute trades to take advantage of the disparity and in doing so, the premiums of the options will be sold back in line. The spread will always have to be executed at a net debit to the investor. The optimum time to execute this spread is when the two calls sold are at-the-money so that the most premium is received. The debit will normally be small, the risk limited to the amount paid for the spread, and the profit limited to the maximum profit of the bullish portion of the spread less the debit. In the above example, if a debit of $1 was paid for the spread, the maximum profit would be limited to $1.50 (25 minus 22.5 minus 1).

Short butterfly spread

A butterfly spread can be sold instead of bought. In this case, the maximum profitability will result when the underlying stock declines below the exercise price of the lowest call sold. Like the long butterfly or sandwich, an arbitrage opportunity may arise when there are pricing disparities between calls. The short butterfly spread will profit if a credit of greater than $2.50 can be received (for a two-and-one-half-point spread) since the maximum loss is $2.50. This would require that the two spreads were executed at different times because no one would ever pay more than $2.50 for a limited profit position of only $2.50.

Condor spread

The condor spread is another variation of the butterfly spread. It involves some modifications to the classic butterfly. The condor consists of the sale (or purchase) of two calls with different strike prices within the purchase of two higher and lower strike calls. For instance, you could buy one $30 call, sell one $35 call, sell one $40 call, and buy one $45 call. Like the butterfly, a loss will occur equal to the debit paid for the spread if the underlying stock advances beyond the higher strike price. Maximum profitability will occur between or at the lower and higher short-call prices. It has a lower risk than the butterfly spread and also a smaller profit potential. The condor spread is rarely used by retail investors.

Box spread

A box spread is another example of a spread that combines two other spreads. A box spread combines both a call spread and a put spread. The spread is either bought, a long box, or sold, a short box.

The following is an example of a long box spread:

Buy one PGS 60 call
Sell one PGS 70 call
Buy one PGS 70 put
Sell one PGS 60 put

The position combines a bull call spread and a bear put spread. Each spread would normally be executed at a debit. The key to this spread is that no matter where the underlying stock trades at expiry, the spread will be worth $10, one of the spreads must reach its maximum intrinsic value. The arbitrage opportunity here is easily seen. If you can purchase this spread for something less than $10, you will have a profit at expiry when the spread matures to $10. Likewise the short box will also profit if the seller can receive premiums in excess of $10, since he will merely have to pay out the equivalent of $10 at expiry.

It will be a very rare event indeed when an investor will be able to execute such a trade for a locked-in profit, especially considering the commissions required for both spread trades. But like the butterfly spread, the box spread shows us the relationship between puts and calls, and how they will combine to define the proper value that they should reflect. Market-makers do not have computer programs to tell them if a particular option is overpriced or underpriced. They use butterflies and boxes to do it for them.

A box spread is essentially a position that locks in a certain profit or loss. Obviously, it is desirable to lock in a profit. Again the theme of arbitrage occurs with this spread. Like the butterfly spread, the box spread will define whether the prices of puts and calls are in line or not. If it is possible to lock in a profitable position, then market-makers will immediately do so. Market-makers also look at a box from the position of buying and selling synthetic stock rather than executing two spreads. Remember option equivalents and conversions. A long call and short put are equivalent to long stock, and vice versa. A market-maker will sell synthetic stock at $70 (the short 70 call plus the long 70 put) in the above example, and buy synthetic stock at $60 (long 60 call plus the short 60 put). He buys stock at $60 and simultaneously sells it at $70, guaranteeing a $10 profit. If he can do this trade for something less than $10 he will have locked in a risk-free profit. The reverse trade is also possible where he may sell the stock for greater than $10 with the knowledge that he will be able to repurchase the position for $10 at expiry. As with other arbitrage situations we have discussed, this opportunity will never actually present itself to the average investor. But it is important to understand these trades so that pricing relationships between different options can be seen.

Ratio writing

Ratio writing is so named because it involves selling options on some other basis than one to one. Remember, covered writing involves buying stock and selling an equivalent number of call options. If you buy 100 shares and sell one call, you are engaged in covered writing. If you buy 100 shares and sell two calls, you have established a type of ratio write. Similarly in a spread, if you sell more calls or puts than you buy you have established a ratio write. In the case of a covered write you have limited risk. When you choose a higher ratio of calls to stock, you suddenly transform the position to one of unlimited risk. One of the calls is not covered and, therefore, has theoretically unlimited risk. Despite this, the strategy is much more common than you might expect.

The delta usually defines the number of additional calls you should sell in relation to the number of calls, or stock, held. For instance, an at-the-money call usually has a delta of close to 0.5, while long stock has a delta of 1. To establish a delta neutral position you would purchase 100 shares of stock and sell two at-the-money calls. The position seeks to reduce directional risk in exchange for volatility or vega risk. It sounds somewhat sophisticated. Does it have an application for the average investor?

Certainly a thorough understanding of delta and naked option writing is essential before you embark on a strategy of ratio writing. But having made that leap, it is possible to dramatically improve the profit potential of an option spread or covered write in return for accepting additional risk. For instance, the call prices of Popular Gold Stock trading at $40 may be as follows:

PGS 40 call	$2.25
PGS 45 call	$0.625
PGS 50 call	$0.125

The normal bull call price spread of purchasing the PGS 40 calls and selling the PGS 45 calls can be done for a debit of $1.625. The cost of this spread can be reduced considerably if one were to sell two or more of the PGS 45 calls for 62.5 cents each instead of the one. A 2:1 ratio spread would cost only $1, and a 3:1 ratio spread would cost only 37.5 cents. Depending upon the particular prices, you can sometimes completely pay for the long call by selling some number of out-of-the-money calls. This is also sometimes known as having calls for free. Of course, they are not really free. The price you are really paying is the risk you assume in writing these additional naked calls.

Several factors must be considered before embarking on this type of strategy. You normally look at the volatility of a stock to determine if a price move beyond a certain point is likely. That is, has the stock historically had this type of trading range? But you should also consider whether it is probable that such a price move will occur. If it is probable, then the strategy is not advisable. In the above example, this would involve a greater than 12.5 per cent price move during the life of the option. Even if such a price move is not likely, you should definitely ensure that there is time to react and close out the offending call position if things do not go your way. Give yourself a mental stop-loss level at which you will close the spread if the stock moves up a certain amount. Accept a small loss to avoid a substantial one. Finally, you should avoid this strategy altogether if you cannot accept the risk of selling naked options.

I have seen another ratio spread used quite successfully. It involves the purchase of a standard price spread and the sale of an additional amount of further out-of-the-money calls or puts. For example, you buy one PGS 60 put, sell one PGS 55 put, and sell one PGS 50 put. At first, there is no risk without a substantial decline in the stock. The position is net short one put with a strike price of $50. But the stock could decline well below $50 without a significant loss occurring. The break-even point is $45 plus the premium for the PGS 60 put, minus the premium for the PGS 55 put, and minus the premium for the PGS 50 put. That is, the position earns a $5 profit once the stock reaches $55. That $5 profit protects the position from loss until the stock reaches $45. Then the break-even point is further reduced by the premium received for the PGS 50 put. Selling the additional out-of-the-money put with a strike price of $50 further reduces the cost of the PGS 60/55 price spread. The probability of a price decline to the break-even point is extremely low. And there should be ample time to react and close the position if things turn bad. In fact, the position should still yield a profit if the stock were to decline as far as $50. At this point you could still close all the puts and exit the position.

A calendar spread can also be executed using some ratio of options sold versus options purchased. In a straightforward calendar spread, a near-term option is sold, and a longer-term option with the same strike price is purchased. The spread is normally executed at a debit. To reduce or eliminate this debit, two or more of the near-term options can be sold for every one of the longer-term options which are purchased. For instance: sell two PGS July 50 calls, and buy one PGS October 50 call. The spread is typically done with out-of-the-money options when you feel it is likely that the near-term options will expire worthless, leaving you with a longer-term call at a considerably reduced price. In fact, for maximum effect you should seek to execute this position at a credit. So when the near-term options expire, a profit has already been made. Again, this strategy assumes the risk of the naked call position until expiry.

One type of calendar spread which was not previously discussed is the reverse calendar spread or back spread. This simply involves the purchase of the near-term option and the sale of the longer-term option. A back spread is not really viable as a stand-alone strategy since it stands to lose in most situations, and especially in a neutral market. Time works against the reverse spreader initially, but eventually works in his favour. Unfortunately, it takes a great deal of time for the spread to profit and the time decay curve works against the purchaser until the near-term option expires. If the underlying stock should advance, then little profit or a loss is achieved since both calls increase in value. A decline is required for the strategy to profit (for calls). There are so many good alternatives available to profit from a price decline that there is no reason here to assume risk of the long-term naked call. Likewise there is no good reason to assume the risks of using a ratio-writing formula in conjunction with this strategy.

Repair strategies

I am not a huge fan of repair strategies since they go against my belief that you should back your judgment when making an investment. If you have purchased a stock and it has declined, then you should consider selling it and cutting your losses. Choose a stop-loss level and exit the position. Admit that you were wrong. However, there are some situations where if you insist on holding a stock that has declined, you can use call options to mitigate your loss.

Suppose you purchased Popular Gold Stock at $50 only to watch it decline to $40. For some reason, you insist on keeping the stock in the belief that it will recover or is worth holding at that level. Part of the investment can be recovered by executing a ratio call spread. In this case, you will not be uncovered on any of the calls you write as in a normal ratio spread because you will use the stock to cover the additional calls you write. Execution of the strategy will also depend upon the prevailing call option prices at the time. The repair strategy works like this: buy one PGS 40 call, and sell two PGS 45 calls. You will effectively have established a covered write as well as a bull call price spread. When I discussed covered writing, I told you not to establish a covered write on a losing stock position simply as a desperate measure. This position assumes that you remain bullish on the stock. The ratio call spread should also be done at virtually a zero, or a very small debit.

Now that you have established the spread, look what happens if the stock recovers half of the decline it suffered. Assume the stock advances to $45 or higher by the expiry of the options. You will have recovered $5 on the stock, but you will also have made a $5 profit on the bull call spread, for a total of $10. This returns you to a break-even point on the original stock position. Even if the stock advances back to your original price of $50, then executing the ratio call spread was worthwhile, except for the commissions. If the stock stays the same, then little is lost and you can try again. Any small advance in the stock up to $45, and the strategy pays off in a big way. You have basically doubled up on the stock position by purchasing an additional call at $40, but you have limited your profit to $5 by the sale of the PGS 45 call.

The one major advantage of this strategy is that it avoids that bane of all investors — the temptation to average down. Averaging down is the practice of continuing to purchase more stock after it has suffered a decline, thereby reducing your average cost. Unfortunately, averaging down involves assuming the risk of a larger stock position. Normally, you don't plan to do this when you begin to buy shares in a company. You buy a stock with the belief that it will increase in value, not decline. Employing the ratio write repair strategy does not add additional risk to the original position, other than the small debit one might pay for the spread. The only risk you have is one that you supposedly were going to assume anyway, the risk of a continued decline in the stock price.

Original strategies

I call this section original strategies to encourage you to use the flexibility of options to build your own investment style. For instance, I have a friend who buys far out-of-the-money puts on stocks where takeover bids have been announced. A stock can advance considerably on the news of a takeover bid. Occasionally lightning strikes and the takeover bid is cancelled. When this happens, my friend's strategy reaps fabulous profits. He typically pays only 6.25 cents for each put option he buys in the hope that the stock will fall several dollars if the takeover fails. To date he has not made a profit, although there have been incidents in the past where he would have. I personally think this is a crazy strategy and basically just a lottery ticket. It is widely speculative. But it is also a very cheap lottery ticket. There is always some chance that the decline will occur, and it is far less risky than selling the stock short. I certainly don't recommend it as an investment strategy, but it is a controlled and inexpensive way to speculate.

The option trading success of Tony Saliba is well documented in the book *Market Wizards*. Saliba used a strategy in his early days that he called "explosion positions." These were positions that had limited risk as well as the potential to profit with an increase in volatility and/or a large price movement. In simple terms this involves buying long-term out-of-the-money puts and calls. However, if nothing happens this can become expensive. To pay for this strategy, Saliba also traded near-term butterfly spreads to take advantage of the time decay. When a large price move occurred, this strategy paid off in a big way .

These two strategies may not have a practical application for the average investor, but they illustrate the flexibility of options. Essentially you can tailor a strategy to fit your own personality and your willingness to assume risk.

CHAPTER 12

Strategies for Index Options

INDEX OPTIONS DESERVE A chapter of their own because of the many different uses they have compared with equity options. Index options also have separate and specific risks that are not found in equity option strategies. Indeed, entire books have been devoted to the subject. Index options share most of the same characteristics of other listed options: limited risk for the purchaser; unlimited risk for the call writer; and similar rights and obligations. But the strategies differ somewhat, both in investment purpose and potential result. Index options are the most heavily traded of all options both in Canada and the United States. They are the most popular of listed options for both the portfolio manager and the speculator. Using index options, a portfolio manager can easily effect a purchase or sale that exposes him to the entire market in a single trade. This obviates the need to make several expensive, risky and time-consuming equity trades. Index options are also used to guard against the systemic risk in a portfolio, when a particular investment may be vulnerable to the movement of the market on the whole.

Why are index options the most popular product traded by retail investors, even though they were designed for institutional investors? There are several reasons for this. Firstly, index options are the most liquid investments trading on an exchange. Secondly, the underlying security of index options, such as the TSE 35 index, is prone to large daily price swings. Finally, an investor need only predict the direction of the market as a whole. You don't need to predict the direction of an individual stock or stock group. In short, index options provide the individual investor with the most bang for his buck.

In general, retail option investors attempt to time the market using index options. It is basically a 50-50 proposition whether the market will go up or down on any given day, and the retail trader may feel that this is his best bet. An index is subject to rather drastic price swings, which can lead to sensational profits if you are on the right side of one of these market moves. Unfortunately, predictions of a market move are not restricted to a period of a month or even a single day. I have seen countless traders buy and sell index options several times during the course of a trading day, changing their position from bullish to bearish. Typically, they also use the shortest-term options in order to obtain the most leverage. Ultimately, they all fail and end up losing most of their portfolio.

For some reason, whenever a trader makes a big profit on the index he is only encouraged to trade it more frantically. I cannot tell you how many traders this has happened to. Believe it or not, I had a client who used a "full moon theory" to trade the market using index options. He began with a $5,000 stake and quickly amassed a large profit of nearly $35,000. Not content with this, or content to return to the size of his initial trades, he began making larger and larger trades until he lost all of his money. The most spectacular example of index options speculation that I have seen involved a young investor who turned $10,000 into $700,000 over a few short months. But he too began to trade larger and larger amounts until his funds were depleted and he ended up actually owing his broker money. I asked the young man if he ever considered pulling back some of his funds to preserve this new-found fortune. He replied that with these huge gains, his earnings no longer represented real money and he was simply caught up in the excitement of the market.

All of this has led me to conclude that these people are at the extreme end of the speculative scale, and must be considered outright gamblers. In fact, The Wall Street Journal reported that the largest number of compulsive gamblers don't gamble in Las Vegas or at the nation's racetracks, but trade with brokers daily in New York and Chicago. I have observed thousands of option accounts on a daily basis and have never seen anyone successful at timing the market. Eventually, all market-timers lose their entire portfolio. I have even seen government economists, convinced they have great insight into the future direction of the market, lose over half a million dollars in under six months attempting to time the market. The real culprit is a lack of money management and discipline. Had these market-timers a real plan or goal in using index options, they would have kept most of their profits and continued to invest at a reasonable level. There is a great temptation to gamble in the options market, but this is simply not the proper way to use options for investment.

Features of index options

Options trade on several indices in North America. The most popular is the Standard & Poor's 100 (OEX) traded on the CBOE. It is American-style exercise. The Standard & Poor's 500 (SPX) also trades on the CBOE, but it is European-style exercise. The Major Market Index (XMI) trades on the American Stock Exchange, and is also European-style exercise. The Toronto 35 Index (TXO) trades on the Toronto Stock Exchange. It too is European-style exercise.

Index options are settled in cash. Upon exercise, the holder of an index option receives the cash difference between the exercise price of the option and the level of the underlying index. With the exception of some long-dated index options, the multiplier is 100. Thus, an option holder who exercises a TSE 35 220 call when the index is at 230 receives $1,000, or 10 multiplied by 100.

Index options also trade on several subindices. This allows an investor who wants to invest in technology stocks to participate in the market without having to choose which stock to pick. It can be very frustrating for an investor to purchase one technology stock only to see some other technology stock experience huge gains. This syndrome, known as "right church, wrong pew," can be eliminated using index options. Options on an index such as the Standard & Poor's 100 are known as broad-based, while those on subindices are known as narrow-based. A broad-based index is by definition more diversified than a narrow-based index. Because of this greater diversity, an exchange does not require as much client margin for a broad-based index transaction.

Special risks of index options

Early assignment. When an index option is exercised, the holder of the option receives the difference between the closing day's index level and the exercise price of the option. The actual level of the index to be used in calculating the value of the exercise cannot be determined until the close of trading on that particular day. This creates a special risk for the index option spread trader that is not present for other classes of options: the changing value of an assignment. If you are assigned on the short side of an option spread, the long side of the spread may not be sold or exercised until the next day, because after being assigned, the markets have closed for the day. By the time the index opens the next morning it may have changed adversely. The actual value of the index when you sell the long side of the spread may drop considerably and the loss can suddenly become much more than simply the difference between the exercise prices.

For instance, suppose you bought an August 440 call and sold an August 445 call to establish a bullish spread. Subsequently, the market rose to some level over 445 and you thought you had realized the maximum return on your spread, $5. However, one day the person you sold the 445 call to exercises his option, forcing you to pay the difference between the market level at the close of trading and the exercise price of your call. Of course, you intend to sell the 440 call to pay for the assignment but you are unable to do so until the next morning. The market opens considerably lower the next day and your 440 call is no longer worth enough to cover the amount you were forced to pay for the assignment of the 445 call. This would not happen with an equity option because you would be assigned, or forced to sell, an appropriate amount of the underlying stock. And you could simply exercise your long call the next day to repurchase the stock at a price $5 lower. Make no mistake, this risk is very real and spread traders should ensure that they are quick to close out the entire spread if there is a possibility of being assigned on the short side of their strategy. I have seen some absolute disasters occur to traders because of this very fact. Remarkable occurrences in the market can cause it to open at vastly different levels on a particular day than the level at which it closed on the previous day. An example of this was the Monday following the U.S. invasion of Iraq where the market moved up some 120 points from its close on the previous Friday

You can expect the purchaser to assign you your obligation when the option that you have sold him has lost its time value. It may even be trading at a discount. This will normally occur in two different situations. The first occurs when the option is very close to its expiry date. The second is when the option becomes very deep-in-the-money and loses its leverage. In these situations, you should expect to be assigned and take some defensive action such as closing your position.

This risk of early assignment can be avoided with European-style options, which can only be exercised at expiry. Both sides of the spread will therefore be exercised simultaneously on the day of expiry. There is no further risk of the market changing because the options have expired.

Uncovered writing. Index options are settled in cash. There is no specific underlying security you can hold that can be delivered in the event of the assignment of a call. The writer of index options must accept an assignment of the cash difference of the exercise price and the index level. Therefore, the risk is truly unlimited. While the risk of selling a put is the maximum value of the index minus the premium received, the enormous value of most indices makes this risk as painful as if it were actually unlimited. Very few investors are properly hedged for an adverse move in the market when they sell index options.

Exercises. The holder of an index option who wishes to exercise does not know what the value of that option will be until the index has closed at the end of the trading day. I mention this as a risk simply to remind you that you should never exercise an index option until the final index level is known. Most brokerage houses will accept exercise notices until 4:30 p.m. on a trading day.

One of the quirks of exercising an index option is the effect of closing the trade. This is in contrast to an equity option where you are usually bullish when you exercise a call, because you are acquiring the underlying stock. In the case of an index option, you don't exercise a call if you are bullish. Your market bias is actually bearish when you exercise a call, and bullish when you exercise a put.

Trading halts. From time to time one stock in an index may be halted. This causes a large swing to occur in the index when the stock reopens for trading. In this case, you do not have a true exposure to the market because it is trading without one of its essential components. For exceptional market circumstances, the entire index may be halted. When the index reopens, it may be at a level vastly greater or lesser than when it closed. Any of these events present special risks to the index trader and especially to the writer of index options. This is largely due to their inability to act on their position while the market, or a particular stock, is closed.

Index strategies for the retail investor

With the frantic use of index options as a speculative tool, it is difficult sometimes to remember that the ostensible use of these products is for hedging market risk. They also allow investors to maintain an exposure to the overall market without risking any significant amount of their portfolio. This is particularly useful when the direction of the market may be uncertain. Let's say you suspect a downturn but you aren't 100 per cent certain. You don't want to liquidate your entire portfolio, but you want some protection should a correction occur. Or, perhaps you don't want to establish a portfolio of equities in a time of market uncertainty, but you also don't want to miss out on any upward market move. You could use index options in either of these situations. In fact, index options were created for these very reasons.

Most of our earlier strategies can be applied to index options. In fact, because index options are the most popular of all options, the market for them is also the most efficient. Their prices accurately reflect the volatility of the market. You will also find that the bid/ask spreads are the narrowest. All of these factors, not to mention their liquidity, make index options one of the most attractive options to use. Unfortunately, most investors use them to implement strategies without having a good idea of how they expect the market to behave. Most investors do not consider the movement of the underlying market beyond a few weeks or so. Again, I must emphasize that the biggest folly the index option trader commits is to attempt to time the market. Time is one of the biggest enemies of the option trader. For some reason investors ignore this risk in return for the large amount of leverage available. Invariably, when you are a great user of leverage, things will eventually turn against you. The proper use of index options follows the basic rules that we have discussed in earlier chapters. It is important to buy options with a longer time to expiry and sell options with a shorter time to expiry. Sure, you will lose some leverage because of the larger cash outlay. But this is far outweighed by the advantage of the slower decay in time value during the near-term life of the option.

Before investing in index options, you should develop your own forecast for the market. Your view of the market should entail sound fundamentals and perhaps some technical considerations as well. It is somewhat outrageous to forecast that "the market will go down today." Or even, "the market will go down in the next four hours." The only time such a prediction would have any certainty is when some major economic news is known in advance. When that happens, you will not be the only one who is privy to this knowledge. The opening prices on index options reflect this news.

Few investors seem to consider purchasing an index put or call in conjunction with the rest of their portfolio. However, this strategy is possibly one of the best non-gambling uses of index options. If your portfolio is composed of several stocks included in an index, an index put is good insurance against disaster. In the event of a large market decline, the index put will offset the loss on the stock portfolio. If you feel the market has advanced too far and is due for a correction you could sell your portfolio and put the proceeds in some risk-free instrument such as a T-bill. However, should the market continue to advance, you will have lost out on a good opportunity for profit. Instead, you should consider buying an index call option in conjunction with your T-bill.

The 90/10 strategy. This strategy suggests that you put 90 per cent of your funds in some money market instrument such as a T-bill, and use the remaining 10 per cent to purchase index call options. The actual ratio of funds maintained in each investment can be altered to fit your market forecast and your tolerance for risk. I prefer the 90/10 ratio because it is conservative enough to give you ample staying power, and fits in with my advice that you shouldn't use more than 10 per cent of your risk capital for one trade. In this case, risk capital is part of a structured portfolio.

Let's say you have a portfolio worth $10,000. The strategy can be used by investing 90 per cent of your portfolio in a T-bill, and the remaining 10 per cent in index options. The return on the T-bill will partially pay for the cost of the call options. If the options expire worthless, then the return on your portfolio will simply be the yield on the T-bill. Assuming a 7.5 per cent yield, your portfolio will be worth $9,168.75. This represents an 8.3 per cent loss, but it is still somewhat less than the 10 per cent invested in index options.

Now think back to our discussion of purchasing calls and the time decay chart. The chart suggested that you did not want to hold calls during their high-decay period – the last 30 days of the option. The 90/10 strategy can be made more efficient and conservative by purchasing a 90-day call option and a 60-day T-bill. At the end of the 60-day period, the call option will rarely be worth zero and some of the investment in it can be recovered. This will significantly reduce the risk of the investment for a small sacrifice in leverage. At the end of the 60-day period, the exercise can be repeated. The calls could be rolled forward or out, by selling the near-term options you own and purchasing another 60-day option. Let's assume that premiums for the at-the-money index calls were as follows:

30-day	$5.875-$6
60-day	$10.125-$10.375
90-day	$14.50-$15.25
120-day	$17.375-$18.50

Assuming the market is stable for the 60-day period, the calls could be sold for $5.875. After purchasing the 60-day call option and holding it for 30 days you would have a loss of $10.3753 minus $5.875, or $4.50. This is somewhat less than the loss you would have incurred if you had simply purchased the 30-day call at $6. The strategy still preserves the main advantages of purchasing call options — limited risk and leverage. It still offers you the potential to reap large gains should the market experience an advance, but your risk is controlled by the limited investment.

Believe it or not, the market will occasionally go your way when you employ this strategy. When it does, you are faced with pleasant choices at the end of the 60-day period. Lets assume that the original portfolio of $10,000 is now worth $11,000. The $1,000 gain is made up of the T-bill yield and the gain in the index options. An aggressive approach would be to adjust the 90/10 ratio to reflect an $11,000 portfolio and maintain a 10 per cent investment in index options. This would require you to buy $1,100 worth of index options and invest the remaining $9,900 in a T-bill. The conservative approach would dictate that you simply continue to invest the original $1,000 in index options and the remainder of your portfolio in the T-bill. You can see that now the yield on the $10,000 will offset a greater amount of the call option purchase. Combine this with the fact that by using a 90-day option for only 60 days, the option will rarely decline to zero. The result is a strategy with a lot of staying power. It will take a long time and a consistently long string of market losses to knock you out of the game.

The 90/10 strategy is a viable and conservative investment approach using index options that the retail investor can readily use as an alternative to a diversified stock portfolio. It also has advantages for investors who want to participate in equities markets but who lack the expertise to pick individual stocks. By definition, this strategy also forces you to be disciplined. It is clearly defined and objective because it is based upon a model. In effect, it is a passive portfolio. It does not require any ongoing investment decisions. A final recommendation to anyone who employs this strategy would be to realign the portfolio once a year to conform to the 90/10 ratio. This requires that you take a conservative approach. Plan to consider the investment as a one-year program, and start fresh each year.

Double write credit spreading. This strategy involves simultaneously writing two separate credit spreads. In theory, it could also be used with a specific equity option, but I have only seen it used in conjunction with an index. Depending upon how conservative you are, the strategy also offers a high probability of success.

Here is how it works:

Index level is 450

Sell one 465 call

Buy one 470 call

Sell one 435 put

Buy one 430 put

You have simultaneously written two spreads for small credits. To a degree it is similar to writing a combination, but with the insurance of buying an additional put and call limiting the loss. At expiry, no matter where the index finishes, only one of these spreads can be in-the-money and for a maximum of $5. The maximum loss, therefore, is $5 minus the credit received for both spreads. The reason I said the strategy had a high probability of success is that it is usually done with options quite far out-of-the-money. In the above example, if the index finishes at or between 435 and 465 you will profit by the amount of the entire proceeds of both spreads. This is also your maximum profit. A range of $30 gives you a pretty good chance of success, but you also receive only small premiums for this degree of comfort. Note also that if the credit received for these spreads is $2 then your break-even points are 433 and 467. So the index can actually finish somewhere around a $34 range before you will begin to lose money.

By bringing in the exercise prices somewhat, say, 440/435 put spread and 465/460 call spread, you can increase the credit you receive but this will also narrow your margin of possible loss to $20 from the $30 in the example. I think you get the idea. You must weigh the amount of risk that you are able to assume in return for the amount of potential gain. You might also factor in the pricing of the various options and attempt to sell the ones that are the most overpriced in relation to the volatility of the index. Finally, you must also consider that this is basically a neutral strategy. It is best used when you believe the index is in a sideways pattern and has no particular direction.

Which options should you write? That's easy. If you don't already know, reread the chapter on selling puts and calls. Obviously, you should sell the options (the spreads) that have the shorter lifetime in order to take advantage of their rapid time decay. I know of one investor who uses this strategy on a monthly basis. He writes two near-month spreads. He generally also attempts to choose spreads that will net him approximately $2 total for both spreads. If the index finishes considerably higher or lower for that month and the spread is in the money, he will lose $3 total. That is his maximum loss, but there are many other possibilities. My friend claims this has been a winning strategy for several years and I do not necessarily doubt him. The reason is because of the laws of probability and our old statistical friend the bell curve. Given the short period of time involved in his strategy, one-month time spans, the market will normally remain within a certain trading range from a statistical point of view. Of course, it will not always do so and may not even do so for several months in a row. So the strategy is not particularly suitable for markets that have a definite trend because of the higher probability of one of the spreads becoming in-the-money.

The real reason for my friend's success with this strategy is his disciplined approach to it. He does the same thing month in and month out and does not get too concerned with his own emotions or views of the market. To that extent, it is an objective strategy. He also manages his money properly so that he can sustain several months of losses in a row without wiping out his capital. I suggest that if you decide to try this strategy you begin with roughly 10 to

15 per cent of your risk capital. Then calculate the loss you might sustain if one of the spreads reaches its maximum intrinsic value at expiry. If the loss is $3, then that amount should not exceed 10 per cent of your risk capital. In other words, if your risk capital is $9,000, then you should not write more than three contracts in each spread, assuming that you are receiving a $2 credit. The potential $3 loss (times 100 x 3 contracts) equals $900, or 10 per cent of your capital. If that does not seem to be a very heavy position to take, remember that you want to use this strategy each month. A 10 per cent loss each month will add up quickly.

A plus to this strategy is the additional return you will be receiving on your capital, assuming you invest it in a T-bill. You also receive interest on the cash credit you receive for writing the spreads. For this reason, the strategy has similarities to the 90/10 strategy where you plan to receive a fixed yield on your capital while participating in the market as a whole. Except with this strategy you anticipate that the market will remain somewhat stable. I must finally point out that your broker will request that you post margin for both of the spreads you write. The margin requirement for a spread is the maximum loss which may result. With a five-point spread, the potential loss is $5 multiplied by 100 multiplied by the number of contracts in the spread. Of course, you may apply the credit received to the margin requirement. It may seem odd that you are required to post margin for both spreads even though you can only lose on one of them, but that is currently what the stock exchange bylaw requires. This is because in a different strategy, such as a box, both spreads can be written when they are in-the-money.

Portfolio simulation

Professionals use the 90/10 strategy in a slightly different manner than the one described above. Portfolio managers purchase an amount of index options that will represent the value of the portfolio. A portfolio with a value of $1,000,000, when the index is at 460, would require the purchase of 22 at-the-money index calls (22 x 460 x 100 = $1,012,000). At a cost of approximately $11.125 a call, the total cost of this transaction is $24,475 (22 x $11.125 x 100). This method does not require an investment of exactly 10 per cent of your entire portfolio in index options, but rather an amount of call options that would represent the performance of a $1,000,000 portfolio. The cost of the index options, $24,475, represents only

2.45 per cent of the portfolio. A T-bill with a 7.5 per cent yield would return $18,291 for a 90-day investment of the balance of the portfolio. The total return of the portfolio for the 90-day period if the options expired worthless would be a loss of $6,183, or 0.62 per cent. If the market advanced during this time, the portfolio would return the gain on the index options in addition to the 7.5 per cent yield of the T-bill.

CHAPTER 13

Strategies for LEAPS

IT IS UNUSUAL THAT A NEW investment tool could be created simply by extending the life of an option. But that is exactly what the CBOE did by creating long-dated options. LEAPS are Long-Term Equity AnticiPation Securities. You will quickly see that the greater amount of time afforded to the LEAPS purchaser dramatically changes the type of strategy they may employ, thus changing the way options have come to be regarded in the marketplace. These options are simply not suitable for the speculator. Those who wish to speculate can choose from the many conventional puts and calls already listed on the options exchange. LEAPS are generally only bought and sold by people seeking a bona fide investment tool. In this chapter, we will be discussing the general features of LEAPS, the pricing problems they pose for the market-maker and the investor, and the way they change the various conventional option strategies. I would also like to acknowledge the advice and support I have received from my colleague Harrison Roth. Those who wish to pursue the study of LEAPS further are referred to his excellent book dedicated to the subject, *LEAPS: What they are and how to use them for profit and protection.*

Features

LEAPS are really not that different from other listed options. They cover 100 shares of stock and can be exercised at any time during the life of the contract. In this respect, they are the same as any other conventional option. They simply have a longer life. The reader may ask, "Isn't a long-term call option simply a warrant?" The answer is, yes and no. A warrant has most of the general properties that a call option possesses: the right to buy a certain amount of stock at a specified price, until a predetermined date. The purchaser pays for the warrant up front and like the call purchaser, has limited risk. There is usually some leverage built in to the warrant because of the lesser amount of capital required for its purchase. But here the similarities end. LEAPS have all of these advantages and many more. First, remember that a warrant is usually issued with the original issue of stock and comes as a unit. Thereafter, no more warrants are issued. There is typically only one warrant trading at any particular time on a given stock. Warrants are only issued by certain companies, as other financing alternatives are available in the marketplace. For these reasons, the number of warrants listed at any given time is limited.

LEAPS on the other hand include both puts and calls on the underlying stock. It would certainly be odd and have very limited benefit to an issuing company to list put warrants on its shares. LEAPS puts and calls continue to be listed on the underlying stock after each expires, and also after the stock has moved a certain amount in either direction. They are a continued investment alternative, unlike the warrant which may have little value after the stock has moved away from the conversion price. There are usually three or four exercise prices for both puts and calls to choose from among the LEAPS listed on any given security.

LEAPS are listed on many of the stocks which also have conventional options trading on them. But given the young age of the product they are not yet available on all listed option classes. LEAPS are listed with a lifetime of usually between 18 months and two years. Unlike conventional options, the expiry month for LEAPS is always January. There are reasons for this. When LEAPS grow to the age where they only have a certain time left (usually nine months), they are rolled into the conventional option classes. In other words, a January 50 LEAP will become a regular January 50 option in the April of the preceding year, nine months before its expiry. This is because there will already be other nine-month options listed on the underlying class and so they are combined into one. After LEAPS are rolled into the conventional series, new series of LEAPS will be listed.

You can see the flexibility of a security that offers a choice of puts and calls with varying exercise prices trading on a given security. You are no longer limited to a strategy covering only nine months, or one type of instrument having only one exercise price . There is nothing immediately mysterious about this product. It simply has a longer lifetime than a conventional option. This simple fact has a dramatic effect on the option strategies you would normally employ.

Buying calls

A quick look at the option quotes in a newspaper will show you the large premiums of at-the-money long-dated options. This immediately discourages many investors from looking further at these options. Remember, the less you spend on an option, the greater the leverage that you will enjoy. If leverage is one of the advantages of buying options then why forfeit this by purchasing a long-dated call? It is a two-way street. You give up some leverage, but you also neutralize that enemy of the option buyer, time.

Whether long- or short-dated, an option still retains the advantages of limited risk. Note from the time decay chart that time value erodes more slowly in a long-dated option than in a shorter one. This is the major advantage of buying a longer-term option than one with less time remaining. Those who use options for solely leverage will not find LEAPS an attractive alternative to purchasing stocks or even conventional options.

Recently, the following prices were available for LEAPS on a well-known stock trading at $29.25 on the Toronto Stock Exchange:

97 LEAP

30 call 3.05 30 put 2.15

25 call 7.125 25 put .50

98 LEAP

30 call 4.20 30 put 3.40

25 call 8.375 25 put 1.00 January (regular series)

30 call 1.20 30 put 1.60

I have intentionally chosen a stock that offers a meaningful dividend yield — 4 per cent. The regular January 30 calls had 180 days to expiry. An additional 365 days of time value could be purchased (the 97 LEAPS) for an extra $2.85. If you were to purchase the rough equivalent of three six-month call options, you would be paying $3.60 rather than the current offered price of the LEAP, $3.05. You would also avoid the additional transaction costs of repurchasing each of the two additional six-month calls. This example was chosen at random and there are other compelling ones available. I suggest that you consider these as an alternative when you are contemplating a long-term program of call buying on a particular stock.

Granted, this is still a considerable amount of time value to purchase. But consider what will happen if you purchase the January 30 call and the stock remains relatively the same. The January call will expire worthless, a $1.20 loss. The 97 January LEAP will theoretically still be worth $2.40, for a $0.65 loss. Remember that the time value of the near-term option will erode more quickly than the longer-term one. This is just another example of how this principle works in practice.

LEAPS allow an investor to make one entrance to the market and hold the position for a considerable period of time. Conventional options must be rolled forward if one wishes to maintain their exposure to a stock with options. This is difficult and expensive. You are always paying for more time each time the option is rolled forward. Transactions will also eat into your profits. But are you making the best use of LEAPS when you buy an at-the-money option? Not necessarily. The best use may be to give up as much leverage as possible by buying a deep-in-the-money call or put.

LEAPS as a stock surrogate

Why buy a stock when you can buy something that is almost as good? Why not buy something that will profit as much as the stock, does not cost as much, and will not lose as much if the stock declines? Sound too good to be true? In-the-money LEAPS offer a sound alternative to the stock purchaser. Of course, you will have to give up something. That something is usually a dividend. You also give up a vote at the annual shareholders meeting. But you will be trading that dividend for the return on the funds that you did not have to commit for a purchase of the stock. You will be trading the dividend yield in exchange for the yield on the funds that can be invested in, say, a T-bill, plus the limited risk feature of the call.

For example, let's say a stock is trading at $30. The dividend yield is 4 per cent, the prevailing one-year interest rate is 6 per cent, and the one-year LEAP with a strike price of $25 is selling for $7. If you were to purchase the stock for $30, you would assume the risks of owning that stock and receive a 4 per cent dividend, $1.20 a share. If you purchase the one-year LEAP for $7, you do not receive the $1.20 dividend but you can invest the remaining $23 at 6 per cent for a $1.38 return. The real time premium of the call is, therefore, $1.82 ($2 - [$1.38 - $1.20]). The LEAP purchaser does not receive the dividend of $1.20, but receives a 6 per cent yield on the funds that were not required for the purchase of the stock, $1.38. The risk for the call purchaser is limited to $7 compared to the stock purchaser who risks $30. And for this, the call purchaser gives up $1.82 in time premium. Is there a real risk of the stock declining below $23.12? If so, then the LEAP is the better purchase. This exercise is a simplistic illustration of the difficulty involved in accurately pricing LEAPS. There is also the consideration that interest rates can change during the life of the option.

Covered writing

I am not going to say much about this strategy since I covered it extensively in an earlier chapter. The mechanics of covered writing do not change when you use LEAPS. The strategy still offers downside protection and increased income, but limits the upside potential of the stock to the strike price of the call that was sold. LEAPS have a much longer time to expiry. This means higher premiums for the covered call writer. So much so that the strategy looks even more attractive than normal. But you have just seen an example of some LEAPS prices that reveal that writing three six-month options will produce more income than writing one 18-month option. You propose the purchases of options with longer expiry dates and must conversely propose the selling of options with shorter expiry dates. The time decay of such a long-dated option makes this strategy somewhat doubtful. Oh, you won't take a beating with it unless the stock tumbles but it is just simply not the best way of executing a covered writing program. When you write an option you want it to expire quickly. Pure and simple. The shorter the option you write, the greater opportunity for profit, again and again. The only real difference when you are dealing with LEAPS is that the premiums are high enough that you will be able to sell a further out-of-the-money call than you might normally have done. This increases your upside potential with the stock, or reduces the limit of your profit on the upside. If you insist on using LEAPS in a covered writing program, then I suggest you use out-of-the-money calls to allow you to profit if the stock advances. If you really want to benefit from using LEAPS in a covered writing strategy then consider calendar spreads instead.

Calendar speads

By purchasing an in-the-money long-dated call you have an effective surrogate for the underlying stock. Many applications using stock with options are available utilizing this surrogate. I call a calendar spread using LEAPS a surrogate covered write. This is because instead of using another option to cover the call you sell in a covered write, you simply use the deep-in-the-money call – the surrogate. This is not the normal application of a calendar spread. Usually you buy an option with the same strike price but a longer expiry date. Nor is it a classic covered write where you purchase the stock. Here you are simply taking advantage of one of the fundamental characteristics of an option, that the time value of the near-term option will erode at a faster rate than the longer-term option. In this case, there is in fact very little time value to the longer-term option. But you can take advantage of the erosion of a shorter-term option just as if you owned the stock.

For example, assume you purchased the one-year deep-in-the-money option described above and sold a 180-day out-of-the-money call.

Stock price is $29.25
Buy one 25 '97 LEAP at $7.125
Sell one January 30 call at $1.20

If the stock has not advanced beyond $30 at the January expiry, then you continue forward and write another 180-day call. If the stock stays the same over the lifetime of the LEAP, then you could at least take in three $1.20 premiums for the three 180-day call options. After exercising your LEAP at the end of the term to buy the stock at $25 and subsequently sell the stock at $29.25, your profit picture would look like this:

Cost of LEAP	$7.125
Minus disposal of stock or LEAP for intrinsic value	$4.25
Loss on LEAP	$2.875
Plus proceeds of selling three 180-day options	$3.60
Total profit	72.5 cents

Not exactly bragging rights I admit. But this is also the least aggressive application of the strategy. Note also that the maximum cost to carry this position is only $7.125 minus the premiums received over time. The funds from the sale of each option amortize the expenditure over time. You have assumed that the stock does not appreciate nor decline for this standstill result. However, you have also not maximized your returns by selling nearer-term options for fastest time erosion.

If the stock begins to creep up, the premiums you receive will also be larger as time goes on. The objective of this strategy is to have the near-term option expire worthless so that another call can be written. The exercise is repeated again and again until the maturity date of the long-term option is reached. It is therefore recommended that you write an out-of-the-money near term call. If the near-term option becomes in-the-money, then you will have realized a useful profit on the long-term call. The near-term option could then be rolled up and out, to capture more time premium, or the entire position closed and the profit taken. A final advantage of the surrogate covered write over the conventional application where you buy the stock is the limited risk of the position. Remember that covered writing offers little protection from a drastic fall in the stock. Using the LEAPS surrogate instead, the loss in this example will be limited to the $7.125 you paid minus the premiums received for the calls sold. This is considerably less exposure than owning the stock at $30.

Pricing and the married put

I have already discussed the possibility of purchasing a put for protection against a possible price decline of a stock that you own. With conventional options, this is not really a viable strategy because it is usually better to simply sell the stock than to pay a premium to hold it. A possible exception is when you owned a stock that had advanced in price. The married put is a strategy where you purchase a stock and simultaneously purchase a put. You may also recall in our discussion on option equivalents the combination of a put plus a stock was equal to a call option. Why go to all this trouble when you could have the same profit and loss potential by simply buying a call?

With LEAPS, buying a put for protection is a viable strategy. The main reason for this is that the lifetime of LEAPS exceeds one year. During this period, a stock decline is possible and some protection becomes desirable. But this strategy is more active by design. On the one hand, it seems a bit odd to want to buy a put on a stock that you are bullish on. For this reason, I am not a huge fan of the strategy. But the intent here is to buy a stock for a period of two years or so, and have the assurance that you will not lose money, only profit. Of course, if the stock remains the same or declines you will have lost the opportunity of investing the funds in some other manner.

The ideal example of a married put would be to purchase a stock at $50 and simultaneously purchase a put with a strike of $50 for, say, $4. Let's assume that the put had a life span of two years, and the stock paid a dividend of 4 per cent. You would then receive $4 in dividends over the course of the two years. The only expense would be the cost of the funds you had tied up in the stock. You would have a virtually risk-free position for free. Does it get any better than this? Of course, there is always the risk that the dividend is cut. If this happened, no doubt the stock would fall and the party would be over. You might sell out the entire position and take your small loss of $4 or so, the amount you paid for the put. This of course would be the perfect conditions to purchase a married put position; also assuming that interest rates were low so the cost of funds was not significant. You will probably not see this kind of opportunity in your lifetime unless you become a market-maker, but I use it as an example to explain the concept. Recall from the chapter on reconversions that having created a free-call option, you could now sell the 50-call option in the market and lock in a profit.

Using the above logic, you can easily determine which is the cheaper investment, the married put or the call. Just do the following math. Take the cost of funds for the time period at the prevailing interest rate. Add the cost of the put. Subtract the dividends you will receive. This gives you the true cost of your married put position. Compare this to the actual premium of the call for the same time period. Which is cheaper? This will tell you if the married put is a viable strategy compared with the simple purchase of a call. As a practical matter, the call will tend to be somewhat more expensive but not by a significant amount.

You can see the effect a change in interest rates may have on the pricing of LEAPS by this example. If rates were to rise significantly, then the cost of the married put would also rise, as would the premium of the call option. The opportunity lost if you invested the funds in some interest-bearing instrument would be more acute. Likewise, an increase in the dividend payment would make the married put less expensive, and the premium of the call would decline. With LEAPS you are dealing with a much longer-term investment than a conventional option. This makes the pricing risks greater for market-makers.

But I must caution that you always be aware in any of these pricing discussions that the prevailing market conditions could account for the variances in prices from what you calculate they should be. The financial health of the company, market sentiment and volatility all play an important role in the behaviour of the underlying security.

Is the married put a viable strategy? Looking at the prices quoted above, the 97 LEAP call is priced at $3.05 and the put at $2.15. With the stock at $29.25, the put already has an intrinsic value of 75 cents, and a time value of $1.40. The call is made up entirely of time value at $3.05. The dividend yield is 4 per cent and both options have 540 days until expiry. Assuming that the risk-free interest rate is 6.15 per cent, we can now do the calculation:

Cost of funds	$269.83
Plus the cost of the put	$140 (time value)
Minus dividends received	$175.50
Equals theoretical price of married put	$234.33

The put option appears fairly priced at approximately $2.15 assuming that the prevailing interest rate is 6.15 per cent. The cost of funds for a one-year period is almost identical to the dividend yield for the 540-day period.

Cost of funds	179.89
Dividend	175.50

In fact, the dividend yield for the 540 days would be identical to a 6 per cent interest rate charged for the funds required to carry the stock, $175.50.

Probably the most incredible thing about this example is that all the numbers are actual quotes. The annual T-bill rate was exactly 6.15 per cent when I wrote this. There are six remaining dividends to be paid before the expiry of the options. It may be an incredible thing to state here but it appears that the market-maker has made a mistake. You could purchase this synthetic call and sell the 30 calls for $3.05 and lock in a risk-free profit of 90 cents. The call is definitely overpriced in relation to the price of the put. Why don't I stop writing this book and rush out to make this trade? I neglected one thing in the cost of these options. The market on the puts was between $1.80 and $2.15, but more importantly the market on the calls was between $2.70 and $3.05. In other words, don't get too ex-

cited. I cannot really sell the calls for the lusty price of $3.05 be-
cause that is the offering price. I will probably have to accept the
bid price of $2.70. That means my little arbitrage will net me a risk-
free 55 cents. After buying 100 shares of stock, buying a put option
and selling a call option, my total transaction costs will far exceed
this 55 cent profit. I will also be tying up my capital in this trade for
quite a long time. Market-makers have more lenient capital requirements for these types of trades and also very low transaction costs.
In the real world, firm traders and market-makers are the only ones
who are in a position to profit from these situations.

Nevertheless, you should definitely consider the married put as
an alternative to a call purchase with LEAPS. You have truly seen
the pricing difficulties you face because of the extended period of
time LEAP calls are dealing with. The major disadvantage to the
married put versus the call option is the lack of leverage and the
capital expenditure. The call will give you much more leverage.
You can purchase almost 10 times as many calls as married puts
with the same capital. Ten call options cost $3,050, which will only
buy one married put. You will have to decide if you are willing to
accept that trade-off: a cheaper call, but less leverage. As a final
note, if interest rates rise then you would have been better off purchasing the call because of the increased opportunity loss of investing your funds in something other than this stock. If rates
decline, then your purchase will look all the better.

Index LEAPS

The main characteristic of an index LEAP is that it covers only 10
times the value of the underlying index. For this reason they are
sometimes known as "reduced-value LEAPS." This is in contrast to
a standard index option which covers 100 times the index. The
multiplier of an index LEAP is only 10 times the premium. The
main reason they are designed this way is to make them affordable
to the average investor. With the standard multiplier of 100, a two-
year at-the-money index option might have a premium of over $100;
making a single option cost $10,000. Few investors would pay this
much for an index option. Indeed, few investors pay for the
reduced-value LEAP. They are simply not that popular as a leveraged investment. An investor is at great risk because of the
enormous time value purchased. They are more popular in the use
of time spreads similar to the surrogate covered write described

above. Of course, you will have to purchase 10 long-term index options for every one near-term index option you sell, since the near-term option covers 10 times the value that the index LEAP covers.

Deep-in-the-money time spreads

A strategy which is gaining in popularity involves using deep-in-the-money European index options. Its popularity stems from the fact that there is no capital outlay involved. That's right. You can employ this strategy without any capital at all. There is no cost to the position nor any margin requirement. Until someone suffers a substantial loss (which is inevitable), it will probably continue to be popular. There are very great hidden risks involved, and I believe the exchanges have been remiss in not devising some capital requirement for the position. The spread is done as any other calendar spread, where you sell a near-term option and purchase a longer-term option. Thus the option that sold is covered for margin purposes. Normally this spread will trade at a debit and require some expenditure on the part of the trader. The deep-in-the-money European options frequently trade at discounts to their intrinsic value, which creates the possibility of doing the spread without any funds. These are the actual prices of some deep-in-the-money index calls on the Standard & Poor's 500 index (SPX).

SPX index level is 562.93

December 625 put	$56.50-$57.50
March 625 put	$54.50-$55.50

Note that the intrinsic value of a 625 put when the underlying index is at 562.93 should be 62.07. In both cases, the puts are trading at a discount to parity. This is largely because, due to their costly premiums, they do not offer any leverage and demand for these puts is low. They trade at a discount because they cannot be exercised; they are European-style exercise. If they were American-style exercise it would be a simple thing to purchase the December put at $57.50 and exercise it for $625, netting the difference between the strike price and the index level as a profit. Obviously, they would not trade at such a large discount if this were possible. This phenomenon makes an unusual strategy possible. You can create a calendar spread for a credit. The December 625 puts can be sold for more than the March 625 puts. The market is not placing any time premium on the March option. Using actual prices, the following trade is possible:

Buy SPX March 625 put	$55.50
Sell SPX December 625 put	$56.50
Net credit	$1

This is the only time a calendar spread can be executed for a credit, with deep-in-the-money European options. The spread is considered covered for margin purposes, and the credit is yours to do with as you wish.

What are the possible profit and loss results for this strategy? To begin with, both the profits and the losses can be extremely large. In practice, a large profit or loss is not very probable but the potential is certainly there. Let's assume that the index stays at approximately the same level or declines. What will happen to the premiums of these puts? Well, nothing much will happen to the March 625 put because it is so far in-the- money no one will want a three-month put with no leverage. But something serious will happen to the December 625 put in the third week of December. It will expire and be exercised for its maximum intrinsic value, $62.07. Remember that this is the option you have sold so you must pay the difference between the exercise price and the index level. If this was an American-style option you could simply exercise the March put to pay for the December put. Why not just sell the March put? Well, of course you can. And that March put will be trading for approximately $56.50-$57.50. You will therefore receive $56.50. After paying for the exercise of the December put, you will have a nasty loss of $4.57. Suppose you sold 10 of these spreads. You will have racked up a fast $4,570 (U.S.) in losses. Using reduced-value LEAPS, this would be divided by 10.

Can this position profit? Yes, of course. You simply need the market to go up. In fact, if the market were to go up to 625 you would have a fantastic profit because the December options would be worth far less than the March. You would receive a credit for selling it, too. Any trade that you can buy for a credit and sell for another credit should no doubt be a winning strategy. But don't get excited, this one's not. It is a terrible strategy and diabolical in that it apparently conceals the true risk. If I buy a call option on the index when it is at 562.93, and the index subsequently rises to 625, I will have made a fantastic profit, perhaps the profit of a lifetime. And I would have known my risk the whole time, that of the cost of the call option. With this deep-in-the-money spread, my risks are indefinite and large losses are possible. If I need the index to rise in order to profit from a strategy, then I will choose one with the least risk and the maximum profit potential. There is a great temptation to trade these spreads because they can be done for "free," and even for a credit. This feature alone makes it very attractive and often leads investors to transact many more spreads than their risk capital can provide for. Do not be deceived by these "free" spreads.

Summary

LEAPS are a valuable new tool that eliminate many of the disadvantages of conventional options. LEAPS offer many possible strategies that are simply not available with other options, warrants or stocks. They fulfill a real need in the marketplace by offering these alternatives. But keep in mind the time-erosion pattern of an option. Near-term options decay more rapidly than long-term options. This allows you to purchase an option for one year, without fearing that it will lose its value by the end of that time. It may still have a year left to expire and still carry most of its value. Because of this time decay feature, the best LEAPS strategies involve long option positions rather than short ones. Covered writing is not nearly as attractive with LEAPS as it is with conventional options. But strategies such as a stock surrogate call and a married put are viable.

CHAPTER 14

Futures Trading

FUTURES TRADING GREW OUT of the practice of forward trading: buying and selling with some agreement on deferred delivery. Originally, futures were designed to accommodate the needs of the agricultural market. Contracts covered grain, coffee, cotton, livestock and so forth. Forward trading began with the cotton trade between the United States and Europe. It took such a long time for cotton to be shipped to Europe that people began arranging for delivery in advance. The risk of price fluctuation was great because of the long delivery and long storage time. With the improvement of storage facilities came the ability to preserve other commodities for delivery in the future. Speculators soon gained an interest in these "to arrive" contracts when they saw the potential for large price changes during the life of a contract. Trading in these contracts increased to a level where a buyer or seller was no longer interested in delivering or taking delivery of the underlying commodity. They simply sought to profit from the price fluctuation of the underlying product during the life of the contract. Eventually a modern commodity market was established to facilitate the trading in these contracts with the founding of the Chicago Board of Trade in 1848.

I have a cartoon on my office wall depicting a fat old stockbroker at a futures firm smoking a huge cigar. He sits behind his desk talking to a worried-looking client and the caption reads, "I've been rich and I've been poor; and it's only 9:30." Like options, futures have come a long way from this stereotype of wild speculation. In fact, futures are more widely used to hedge large portfolios than options. The reason for this is the large contract size and the liquidity of the market. A futures contract on the Standard & Poor's 500 index covers 500 times the level of the index. The option on the same index covers only 100 times the cash value. For the portfolio manager it is much cheaper and easier to effect a transaction in the futures market than hundreds of individual trades on the stock exchange.

A future is defined as "an agreement between a seller and a buyer to exchange a predetermined amount of an underlying security, for a specific price, at a stated date in the future." The key difference between a future and an option is that a futures contract is an obligation on the part of both the seller and the buyer. The seller must deliver the amount stated in the contract at the specified price and the buyer must take delivery of that security. For this reason, the risk is essentially the same for both the buyer and the seller. This is in contrast to option trading where the greater risk is assumed by the seller of the contract.

Features

Futures differ from options in many other ways. Listed options have standardized features, but this is not the case with futures. A futures contract on corn will cover a different quantity of the underlying interest than pork bellies or lumber. Quality is another important consideration to a futures contract. Commodity contracts in particular normally prescribe that the product must be of a certain standard. The only listed options that carry this requirement are gold and silver which specify that the underlying metal must be 0.999 per cent fine. In order to prevent trading abuses in the futures markets, the exchanges establish limits on how many times a single contract may change hands on any given day. These limits differ for each individual commodity.

Hedgers and speculators

The concepts of speculating and hedging are more prevalent in futures trading than in options. If you are a supplier or purchaser of a commodity, then you may have a bona fide economic need to use a futures contract. A grower of corn, for example, may wish to lock in the price he will receive for his crop. And he will agree to deliver it at some future date for a predetermined price. The purchaser of that futures contract may have some real use for the commodity or he may simply be speculating that the value of that crop will increase during the life of the contract. It is rare that some other unaffected individual will need to use that futures contract as an investment. There is little ground between the speculator and the hedger in the futures market.

Today most futures trading activity surrounds the trading of contracts on financial instruments. The large amounts of government-issued securities have created a need for buyers and sellers to have a fast entrance or exit from this market. Large financiers of government debt also seek some way to hedge away the risk of holding these instruments. Instead of buying or selling $1,000,000 worth of Government of Canada bonds, an investor needs only to buy or sell one futures contract on the Montreal Exchange. Because of the large size of these contracts and the relatively small amount of capital required to purchase or sell them, futures afford the investor a great deal of leverage. For the speculator, leverage is the most appealing feature of a futures contract.

Some basics

When you purchase or sell a futures contract you are committing to deliver or take delivery of the underlying commodity or security. In practice, one will rarely do this. The contract will normally be closed in the secondary market prior to its expiry, unless you are in a business that has an industrial or commercial use for the commodity. Your broker will give you many warnings to close out the contract before the delivery date.

The spot price is the current price of the underlying security. The underlying security of a futures contract is also known as cash. It is known as cash whether it is a contract on corn, oil or an actual currency. The spot month is the current month and the spot contract is the current month contract. The market for the actual commodity or underlying security is known as the cash market.

The predominant feature of a futures contract is the leverage it affords. For instance, you can purchase a contract to take delivery of an amount of corn in December for a fraction of the actual value of the amount to be delivered. A Canadian dollar contract covers an underlying amount of $100,000. There is a risk that the dollar may fluctuate up or down after you have assumed the obligation to purchase it. Your broker will ask for some security against this event in the form of margin. The margin for a Canadian dollar contract will be approximately $850 (U.S.). Thus, when you purchase a Canadian dollar contract, you must deposit at least $850 (U.S.) in your account on the day of the trade. Subsequently, each day your broker will mark your margin account to market and make an adjustment to your cash account for an amount equal to your profit or loss on the contract. For example, let's say you buy one December Canadian dollar contract at 74.14 cents (U.S.). The next day the Canadian dollar falls to 73.89 cents (U.S.), and your account is debited $250 (U.S.). The following day the Canadian dollar advances to 74.69 cents (U.S.) and your account is credited $800 (U.S.). And so forth. You can see how quickly money can be made or lost in the futures market depending on how many contracts are purchased or sold.

Many of the strategies discussed with options trading can also be applied to futures. Spreads are common but typically involve the buying of one type of commodity and the selling of another. For instance, you might purchase a contract to deliver wheat in December, and at the same time, write a contract to sell corn in December. The difference in prices is the spread. You will be hoping that the price of the spread advances, either that wheat advances in relation to the price of corn or that corn declines in relation to the price of wheat.

You can also effectively perform a covered write in the futures market, though it is actually known as a hedge. If you are the owner of a commodity, you can sell a future on it to lock in a specific price for delivery at some later date. There is very little additional income derived from doing so, but as the holder of the commodity you are guaranteed some price in the future. There is very little risk in selling the futures contract since you have the underlying security to deliver. You will not be subject to the losses of the short futures contract, but you will have forfeited the profits you would have made on the underlying security had you not sold the futures contract. In return, you are assured a certain price and are not exposed to a price decline in that security.

Options on futures

It may sound complex to have options trading on futures, but the concept is really quite simple. (And no, there are no futures trading on options.) In this case, the underlying interest of the option is a futures contract. Options on futures can prove to be especially useful in situations where there are not options trading on a particular security. For instance, a farmer who wishes to obtain some protection from an adverse price movement in a crop may wish to purchase a put option. However, there are very few others who wish to trade options on, say, corn or wheat. But there are many who trade corn and wheat futures. This creates a liquid market for these securities. Futures contracts give the farmer only the choice of buying or selling his crop for future delivery. He may simply want some price protection and the opportunity to continue to profit from a price advance in his commodity. By purchasing a put option on a futures contract he has the right to sell a futures contract at some later date. If the price of his underlying commodity increases, he may choose to do nothing with his options contract and sell the commodity at the more favourable price.

Options on futures afford the investor the same advantages as conventional options: the right but not the obligation to buy or sell a stated amount at a predetermined price, until a specified date in the future. Options on futures also afford the speculator the opportunity to avoid the risks associated with directly purchasing a futures contract. They are not obliged by the contract. They have limited and known risk, but can profit from a directional move in the underlying futures contract and, indirectly, from the underlying security of that futures contract.

There are many peculiarities to futures options not found in conventional options. The expiry date of the futures option will normally occur prior to the expiry date of the underlying future. This is to allow for the exercise of the option in time to meet the delivery date of the future. However, this is not true of all futures options. Some, like the Standard & Poor's 500 option future, expire at the same time as the underlying future. There is no automatic exercise of futures options contracts. You must be especially careful to note the expiry date of your futures option in order not to miss out on a possible profit. Your broker should notify you of this event but you should be aware of it for your own protection.

Futures options require a different level of sophistication than conventional options. Futures options are traded in a futures account and by a futures broker. Therefore, an investor must be familiar with futures trading and the risks associated with them before embarking on an investment strategy involving futures options. You should only be using futures options if you are experienced with trading futures and can afford the losses associated with them.

CHAPTER 15

Other Derivatives and the OTC Market

THIS CHAPTER COVERS OTHER types of derivative products that are listed on an exchange but do not fall under any other category. It will also briefly describe the over-the-counter (OTC) market which appears in the news so often these days. The OTC products, such as swaps, are generally what the press is referring to when they write about "derivatives." Many of the listed derivative products use some of the main concepts of options or futures. Others are known as basket products. Basket products take their name from the fact that they derive their value from several securities packaged together in a basket, such as an index. Some of these basket products have options available on them.

Caps

Caps are derivatives that consist of an index spread with a predefined margin of potential profit or loss. Caps are traded on the Chicago Board Options Exchange and are currently only available on index options. Caps may be a call cap or a put cap and can be bought or sold. If you buy a call cap with a strike of $500, you are effectively establishing a spread as if you bought $500 call and sold a $530 call. You have purchased a 30-point call spread with one easy transaction. Your profit and loss are limited as with any spread. If the index declines below 500, your loss is limited to the amount you paid for the cap. If the index advances above 530, your profit is limited to the difference between the cap strikes of $500 and $530, minus the amount you paid for the cap.

If you sell a $500 call cap, then you have effectively sold a $500 call and purchased a $530 call. You have created a bearish call price spread with a single transaction. The loss is limited to the difference between the cap strikes minus the premium received. And the profit is limited to the amount you received for selling the cap. The appeal of cap is that they can be transacted as a single purchase or sale, in contrast to a spread which involves two transactions, and often two commissions. A spread cannot always be executed at a desired price because the spread price is not always known.

Caps have an important feature called mandatory early exercise. If the index closes above 530, then the $500 call cap is immediately exercised. Three thousand dollars (the difference between the strike prices) is paid to the holder of the cap, and debited from the seller of the cap. Caps are European exercise. They can never be exercised during their lifetime unless their maximum intrinsic value is reached. Note also that the index must close at or above the higher strike of the cap in order for the cap to be exercised. The cap will not be exercised if the index only trades above the strike during the day and later closes lower than the higher strike of the cap.

The option exchanges have developed caps and other derivatives with unique features in order to accommodate the needs of investors who were trading similar products in the over-the-counter market. Caps replace the conventional spread and do not involve a short option. For this reason they are allowed to be purchased in a cash account. This feature accommodates the needs of certain institutional accounts, like pension funds, that are not allowed to purchase securities on margin. As over-the-counter options trading booms, you can expect to see the exchanges develop more products to compete for this business.

PEACS and SPECS

PEACS (payment enhanced capital security) and SPECS (special equity claim security) are issued by the Canadian Split Share Corporation and trade on the Montreal Exchange. They are basically what the company's name implies, a split share. One PEAC and one SPEC are equal to one share. Together, they can be exchanged for the underlying share at any time. The selling institution actually holds the underlying shares in trust for the investor should this event occur. PEACS and SPECS are typically issued with a five-year expiry.

The PEAC offers the purchaser the dividend yield of the underlying security, plus a limited capital gain in the event of an increase in the stock. The capital gain is limited by a predefined crossover point. Sound familiar? It is effectively a covered write on the underlying security. It offers a defined yield, small upside potential with limited risk. A PEAC's attractiveness lies in the ability to purchase this covered write with a single purchase, usually requiring less capital than fully paying for the underlying shares and selling a call.

A SPEC is the second split portion of a security and offers the investor participation in an advance in the underlying security. In this respect, it has many similarities to a warrant. A predefined termination claim price represents the value of the SPEC at its expiry. SPECs offer leverage, limited risk and theoretically unlimited profit.

TIPS

TIPS is an acronym for Toronto Index Participation Securities. They trade exclusively on the Toronto Stock Exchange. TIPS are a basket security. A TIPS unit consists of 1/20th of the value of the Toronto 35 index. If the index is trading at 200, the index is worth $20,000, and a TIPS unit is worth $1,000. Therefore, 20 TIPS units would represent 100 shares of each stock in the index. TIPS allow you the opportunity to purchase a basket of all the stocks making up the Toronto 35 index, in a single transaction. Owners of TIPS units are also entitled to the dividends that all of the stocks collectively pay. The collective dividend yield of the Toronto 35 index is paid to TIPS holders on a quarterly basis. You can purchase a broad exposure to the index and diversify your holdings with TIPS. They are also eligible for self-directed registered retirement savings plans. TIPS were designed to compete with the many index mutual funds available and their liquidity allows you to easily enter or exit the Toronto 35 market. A trust company holds the equivalent amount of securities to the number of TIPS issued. This means that a holder of a large number of TIPS can actually redeem the units for the equivalent number of underlying shares.

Index options can also be written against the TIPS units, although it requires 20 units to completely cover one Toronto 35 index option. An alternative is to use TIPS options. A TIPS option has essentially the same terms as an equity option and covers 100 times the value that the TIPS units trade for in the market. However, because the units trade at 1/20th of the value of the actual index, the volatility of the units is extremely low. This results in very low premiums for the TIPS options, making strategies such as covered writing unattractive.

HIPS

HIPS is an acronym for hundred index participation securities and is another basket security listed on the Toronto Stock Exchange. Like their sister product TIPS, they represents an interest in the shares comprising an underlying index. In this case, it is the TSE 100 index. HIPS pay collective dividends just like TIPS. HIPS are eligible for self-directed registered retirement savings plans, too. The market value of a HIPS unit is approximately 1/10th of the value of the underlying TSE 100 index. Like TIPS, HIPS can be redeemed for the underlying shares if you hold a certain amount of the security. HIPS and TIPS both offer you an opportunity to participate in the market as a whole without making many individual purchases or purchasing an index fund.

SPDRs

SPDR is an acronym for Standard & Poor's despositary receipt. They are colloquially known as spiders. They are a basket of securities representing the Standard & Poor's 500 index. Like TIPS and HIPS, SPDRs allow you to participate in the underlying index without buying every stock in the index, or buying an index mutual fund. They are very liquid and trade on the American Stock Exchange. SPDRs pay a proportionate amount of the dividends paid by the stocks on the index, on a quarterly basis. One SPDR is normally worth 1/10th of the value of the Standard & Poor's 500 index.

Flex options

Flex options are designed to capture some of the customized option market which trades largely over-the-counter. The average investor need not be too concerned with them since they involve large and unusual positions designed to fulfill some very special needs. There is no specific underlying interest to a flex option. They are basically anything that a large institutional investor may want at any particular time. Orders for flex options are passed to the trading floor in terms of what the investor is actually looking for. Institutional investors are looking for strategies with non-standard time frames. They are often looking for a specific expiry date for a strategy such as a collar on the Standard & Poor's 500 index. These combinations of puts and calls with non-standard strike prices and expiration dates are then bid on by various market-makers on the floor of the exchange. The price is not known until the order is put up for auction. The investor decides if that price coincides with his needs or goals.

The OTC market

Unless you are a corporate user of swaps or actually enter the business of trading over-the-counter derivatives, you will probably never encounter these products. This section will give you an idea of the scope and flexibility of these products. For instance, how would you like to hold an option for six months, and then decide whether it will be a put or a call, regardless of what price the underlying security is trading at. This is possible with OTC options. Needless to say they are the most sophisticated of options. That is not to say that they must be complicated. Many are really just your garden-variety forward contracts used by corporations to hedge their risk, often in the foreign exchange market. For each of the following examples, assume that you are a large corporation or an institutional investor (such as a mutual fund) with complicated financing needs, and that you seek to customize the investment to suit your portfolio.

Swaps

Many of the options traded in the OTC market are known as plain vanilla swaps. There is nothing really complicated about them. A swap can be a straightforward agreement to trade one currency for another, one portfolio for another, or even a specific yield for some other investment. Let's assume you are a large corporation with floating-rate debt outstanding. For various reasons, you seek to limit your exposure to interest rates by converting your debt to a fixed rate. By simply swapping your floating-rate debt for fixed-rate debt you can avoid the expense or penalty associated with repurchasing the existing instruments and reissuing new debt instruments. An OTC dealer will perform this swap for you at some fee which will represent a substantial savings for you over the cost of converting the existing debt in some other fashion.

Institutional investors often need to switch a portion of their portfolio from one instrument to another. The size of these transactions makes them expensive and cumbersome. To avoid these problems, institutional investors use the swap market to perform such a simple swap as the yield on a $100,000,000 bond portfolio for the yield on an equity portfolio of comparable size.

I recently analyzed a mutual fund portfolio that actively utilized currency swaps. Sound risky? It wasn't any riskier than their investment in some foreign bonds. They were engaging in a type of currency arbitrage. Let's say the yield on the 30-day U.S. treasury bond is 8 per cent. The fund would attempt to outperform this yield by purchasing foreign bonds that had higher returns. The problem with doing this was that they were vulnerable to the foreign exchange risk of the currency they purchased. They did not want to risk suffering a loss on some currency but wanted to profit from a higher yield. That's easy. All they had to do was just purchase a foreign bond and at the same time make an agreement to exchange the principal dollar amount of the bond for an equal amount of U.S. dollars at a time in the future – the maturity date of the bond. You convert your U.S. dollars now to purchase the bond, and agree to swap back the foreign currency in the future at an equal conversion rate. Now you do not really care what happens to the conversion rate between U.S. and foreign dollars because your exchange rate is locked in. You have avoided the risk of a decline in the foreign currency but you can enjoy the higher yield it offers. It is an arbitrage trade of sorts because you are taking advantage of the swap market to outperform U.S. bond yields. There are many other swaps available that may be contingent on some other event. The agreement to swap currencies may depend upon interest rates reaching a certain level. The possibilities are almost endless.

When you see the press preaching about the evils and risks of derivatives, they are usually talking about the over-the-counter market. Of course, there are many types of derivatives, both listed and unlisted, that have been trading for years. The recent uproar over derivatives trading is mainly directed at the treasury departments of large institutions that employ these products to control specific risks. For some reason, the public perceives these instruments as a great evil in our society despite the fact that greater losses have occurred in other financial areas such as real estate and savings and loan institutions. I recently watched a special on derivatives on the television show *60 Minutes*. The entire focus of the show was the lack of knowledge people had about these products. No doubt. But there are many people who do understand derivatives and use them effectively every day. Suffice it to say that whenever someone uses leveraged products on an unhedged basis, there are sure to be some big losses. Most of the losses that have hit the press in the past five years happened because the positions were not truly hedged, and the risk was open-ended. Losses have also resulted from specific individuals trading counter to their customer's or their firm's objectives. The recent collapse of Barings PLC was the direct result of an individual trading without proper supervision. In fact, the derivatives he traded were simply listed futures on the Nikkei index. They were not complex at all, and were definitely not to blame for the collapse. He could just as easily have bought a single stock, only to have that stock plummet in value.

There are many risks that are unique to the OTC market. You will probably never come across them. When you make an option transaction, a clearing corporation guarantees the contract. In the OTC market, the only guarantor of the contract is the person you make the trade with. This is known as counter-party risk. There is also pricing risk, legal risk and liquidity risk. The greatest risk in the OTC market, in my opinion, is that of supervision or the lack of it. In at least two of the recent major derivatives fiascos, the culprit has been an individual trader who sought to conceal trading losses. This resulted in the individuals trading more heavily in the hope that they could recover these losses and avoid embarrassment or dismissal. The result was financial ruin. The theme of controlling risk and taking small losses to avoid large ones is just as critical in the OTC market as it is in the listed options market. Clearly a firm should have strong audit controls to prevent any one individual from trading enormous, unhedged or leveraged positions.

CHAPTER 16

How the Business Works

NOW THAT YOU KNOW THE strategies, it's time to get them working for you. This chapter will give you a brief overview of the options markets in Canada. It is intended to give you a head start on how to open an account, what types of orders you can place, and some practical advice on things like margin and commissions. While the trade volumes in Canada pale in comparison with those in the United States, options are by no means an insignificant part of the Canadian investment community. The lack of volume can pose liquidity problems for the investor. To counter this, the exchanges operate a market-maker system that guarantees you will always be able to buy or sell 10 contracts on the bid or offer. This will usually be a sufficient quantity for the average investor. In addition, independent competitive option traders also trade for their own accounts on the exchange floor. This helps improve liquidity, too. But the spreads between the market quotations can often be a deterrent to trading options in a particular series. When this happens, do not accept an inferior price just for the sake of executing your trade. Offer or bid for your option at the price you wish. Do not be disappointed if your order is not filled. There are hundreds of stocks and options listed from which to make another investment choice. After all, the price that your option trade is filled at should be essential to your investment strategy. A disciplined and patient choice will usually be the best one.

Opening an options account

Options are highly regulated in Canada. The securities commissions, stock exchanges and Investment Dealers Association have strict rules about how a firm conducts its options business. To begin with, a firm must receive specific formal approval to be in the options business. To get this approval a firm must satisfy several conditions. These conditions include procedures to ensure that every client who trades in options is given a risk disclosure document as well as an option trading agreement. The disclosure document is a pamphlet similar to the prospectus you receive when you purchase a mutual fund. This document, the Summary Disclosure Statement For Exchange Traded Options, outlines many of the risks associated with trading options. The options trading agreement outlines a firm's policy regarding things like assignment methods and margin.

Most investment firms are equipped to trade in options. This means that they are licenced to do so by securities regulators. In order to be licenced, various personnel in the firm must pass several securities exams and be registered with an exchange. Your broker must also have passed the Canadian Options Course and be registered as a Registered Options Representative prior to accepting any options trades from you.

The regulators of the industry recognize that options have special risks and require a degree of skill and knowledge to trade them. You will therefore find that your broker may advise against you using options, or not allow you to open an options account at all. This will depend largely on your experience as an investor and your ability to assume risk. In order to determine this, your broker will give you an options application to complete, as well as an Option Trading Agreement and a risk disclosure statement.

Order entry and trade execution
A market-maker will guarantee to fill an order of up to 10 contracts on the bid or offer. This varies slightly from exchange to exchange, but most have a minimum guaranteed fill rule of 10 contracts. Because of that guarantee, market-makers will not necessarily post your bid or offer if it is for a lesser amount and between those markets. For example, the market on a particular option may be $1.50-$1.75. You want to purchase five contracts at $1.60. The trader will book your order and the market will not change. This is because the market-maker would be obliged to fill the other five contracts (up to 10) if he posted your bid for five. (The Montreal Exchange has a rule that the market-maker must either fill an order for less than 10 or change the market to reflect the order.) Do not be too alarmed at this, your order will still be filled if it can be matched with another order, or if the market on the option changes so that it is matched by the bid or offer.

Many investors believe that they should enter orders with special terms associated with them to ensure that the orders are filled the way they want them to be. If you specify "all or none," you are asking that the entire order be filled or none of it. If you specify "minimum fill," you are asking that a minimum number of contracts be filled or none at all. These requirements make your order more difficult to trade, and your order becomes the last priority on the trading floor. Without some luck, your order will never be filled. Although you will never get a partial fill on an "all or none" order, most brokers will usually not force a partial fill of one contract on their clients. I strongly discourage you from placing these restrictions on your orders. You will find that your orders are filled more frequently if you place them without restrictions.

Commissions

Commissions are really not too mysterious. They are the fee your broker will charge you in exchange for his advice and for executing a trade. Since commissions were deregulated, brokers can now negotiate the amount they charge. Previously, commissions were standardized. A broker was forced to charge a fixed commission and negotiation was not possible. Now competition reigns, and commissions will vary from broker to broker. As well, discount brokers have sprung up across the country.

Prior to deregulation, it was difficult and expensive to execute certain types of option trades, particularly spread orders. This was because a commission was charged for both sides of the spread order. Now some brokers only charge you one commission for the entire order. This has made the spread a much more viable strategy than it was previously. In fact, most contingent type orders can be executed for one total commission, including a "buy write," an order to simultaneously buy a stock and sell a call. Check with your broker to ensure that you get the best deal possible.

Margin

Margin is basically good faith money or security that you must post with your broker when you make a trade. If you have paid for a trade in full, then there is no further margin requirement because there is no further risk than the amount already paid. But many trades involving options involve some additional or unknown risk during the life of the contract. For instance, when you sell a naked call option you have assumed the risk of a theoretically unlimited loss. You cannot expect a broker to assume this risk on behalf of his client, and in fact the exchange will not allow him to do so. Other positions, such as short stock, spreads and all short options, require margin. In these cases, your broker will ask that you post some amount of capital in the event of a loss. He requires some assurance that you will have the means to pay for any losses that may result.

Margin also serves other purposes in the industry. An exchange dictates that there are minimum amounts of capital that must be posted for different transactions. This has the effect of creating a level playing field for all the participants. No one is exempt from margin requirements. Margin also ensures that investors do not trade beyond their means. If you do not have the capital for a trade, your broker will not execute it for you.

Finally, margin can present a type of risk to any trader. If a stock or option moves adversely then your broker may request that you post additional margin. In the event that you do not have any more capital to post with him, your position may have to be closed out. In fact, your position may even be closed out without your knowledge and at a disadvantageous price if your broker cannot contact you. This may result in a loss for you where none need have occurred. If you are unable to capitalize your positions then you are basically over your head. If you always ensure that you will have enough margin to withstand an adverse price move, this risk will never concern you.

Margin requirements

Here are the current Canadian exchange minimum margin requirements. These requirements change from time to time. They may also differ slightly from American requirements. Some brokers will request slightly more than the exchange requirement, or even a minimum account size before they approve an account for such trades as naked writing. Remember, these guidelines are only the minimum. Always check with your broker to ensure that you understand the amount of margin necessary for a trade.

Long stock, option eligible	30 per cent
Other stocks trading over $2	50 per cent
Stocks trading $1.75-$1.99	70 per cent
Stocks trading $1.50-$1.74	90 per cent

Short stock, option eligible	130 per cent
Other stocks	150 per cent

Long equity call/put Payment in full of the option premium.

Short equity call/put 25 per cent of the market value of the underlying security plus 100 per cent of the option premium (marked to market) minus any amount the option is out-of-the-money. Minimum is 5 per cent of the market value of the underlying security plus 100 per cent of the premium.

Short bond call/put 3 per cent of the market value of the underlying security plus 100 per cent of the option premium (marked to market) minus any amount the option is out-of-the-money. Minimum is one-half per cent of the underlying security plus 100 per cent of the option premium.

Short index call/put 10 per cent Canadian or 15 per cent U.S. of the market value of the underlying security plus 100 per cent of the option premium (marked to market) minus any amount the option is out-of-the-money. Minimum is 5 per cent of underlying index plus 100 per cent of the premium.

Short straddle/combination The greater of the margin requirement for either the short put or short call, plus any amount by which the other short option is in-the-money. There is no deduction for the out-of-the-money amount of the short option with the lesser requirement.

Spreads Debit spreads require only that the purchaser pay for the spread in full. Credit spreads require that the writer post an amount equal to the difference in the exercise prices, or the amount of margin required for the short option, whichever is less.

Butterfly, sandwich, box or condor spreads Each spread in the strategy must be margined individually.

Long stock + short call The loan value allowed is 70 per cent of the lower of the market value of the stock or the exercise price of the call.

Long stock and long put 25 per cent of the market value of the long stock plus 100 per cent of the premium of the put plus the lower of 5 per cent of the market value of the stock or the out-of-the-money.

Short stock + short put 130 per cent of the greater of the market value of the short stock or the exercise price of the short put. There is no margin required for the short put.

Short stock + long call 125 per cent of the market value of the short stock.

Long caps 100 per cent of the premium of the cap.

Short caps The difference between the caps strikes (usually 30 points or $30). The premium received for the cap may be applied to the margin, as in a credit spread, but must be left in the account. The amount of margin may not exceed the amount it would require to margin a short index option with a strike of the lower exercise price of the cap in the case of a call cap, or the higher exercise price in the case of a put cap.

Short cap straddle The total of the differences between the strike prices of each cap sold (30 + 30) minus the premiums received for both caps. Note that you cannot sell two caps and only post margin for one on the logic that you will only lose on one of the caps sold. Theoretically, one side could reach its maximum intrinsic value and be exercised, only to have the market reverse drastically the next day and the other side reach its maximum intrinsic value.

Other margin requirements

In order to be considered covered in a spread, the long option must not expire before the short option. If the long option expires first, then the normal margin for a short call or short put applies. In any combination where two spreads compose a strategy, such as a butterfly or box, the spreads must be margined separately and cannot offset one another, even though the maximum loss of the entire position may be limited. Other combinations of securities that are convertible into the underlying stock and a short call are possible and may be considered covered. These include: warrants, preferred shares, convertible debentures and instalment receipts. Margin requirements vary from broker to broker, and can also be changed by the industry at any time. Check the margin requirements of your strategy with your broker before entering into a trade.

Exercises and assignments

I have already discussed many of the risks associated with exercises and assignments in previous chapters, but I think it is worthwhile to review them here. Your greatest risk is of early assignment, or being assigned at a disadvantageous time. I would like to add here that most brokers will also charge you a commission for this assignment. If you exercise an equity option and purchase the underlying stock you will probably be charged a commission similar to the one you would pay for buying the stock. You may want to avoid this additional cost and simply close out your option if you think you are likely to get assigned. Remember that assignment is most likely to happen when an option is deep-in-the-money, has little or no time value and is close to expiry. It may also occur when the holder of the option wishes to receive a dividend that is due on the underlying stock. You should keep aware of when an assignment is likely and take defensive action.

A plan of action

With so many strategies to choose from, no one strategy will best suit all investors. It will take some time to discover what strategy works best for you. It will usually serve you well to stick with a strategy that you fully understand and are comfortable with. I have one friend who only uses covered writing. Other friends use a put selling program and some simply buy calls. Understanding a strategy means that you are aware of what the underlying stock must do for your strategy to be successful. It also means that you are aware of any special risks that are associated with the strategy. With sound product knowledge, you will be able to sleep at night. Most brokers are happier with clients who understand how the market works. It makes their job simpler and they can be content that you are aware of the risks and responsibilities you must assume.

CHAPTER 17

Some Words about Discipline

ENTIRE BOOKS HAVE BEEN devoted to the subject of the psychology and discipline of trading the stock market. I have touched upon the subject of psychology and discipline at various times in past chapters but I feel it merits one last look. Until you learn to view the market as a totally detached phenomenon, you will never be a successful trader. It would seem obvious that your personal views of the market will have no bearing on what actually transpires. Yet day after day, investors insist that they cannot be wrong and the market will behave a certain way rather than taking the time to notice what it is actually doing. Make no mistake, it is much easier said than done. For some reason it is more difficult to acknowledge that the market is in a steady uptrend, rather than to assume that it must eventually come down.

Pay attention to the market

A friend of mine once made a considerable amount of money betting on a roulette wheel. He simply bet that the number would be red (a slightly less than 50/50 proposition). Now, on a roulette wheel there are 18 red numbers and 18 black numbers; as well as one or two green numbers. So to continually bet one colour and to continue to win is quite incredible. After the colour red had appeared eight times in a row, people kept telling him how crazy it was to keep betting on red. Their logic was "Eventually black has to come up." Well they continued to lose their money and my friend continued to win. Why? It has nothing really to do with whether the odds favour red or black. The odds on the spin of a roulette wheel do not change. They are the same each time the ball is spun; equally in favour of red or black. So what can you deduce when red comes up eight times in a row if the odds of red appearing again are the same as before? There is one thing that you may have noticed here.

My friend was on a "streak" of reds. Nothing more and nothing less. If you were actually watching what was happening you would say: "There is an incredible streak going on at the roulette wheel." The losing attitude would be to say "Eventually black will come up so I will bet black." Those who took this view suffered through an additional six losses on the wheel before black appeared. People were truly amazed that someone could actually have bet red so many times in a row and won each time.

Of course, my friend could well have quit if he had lost that second spin because he could see that there was no trend; or if he was unable to identify the trend. Assume that the market is close to a 50-50 proposition at any given moment. It may go up or down. The odds remain the same no matter what time you choose to enter into a transaction. If a stock is experiencing a dramatic and continued price move, it would be folly to assume that, at any given point, that advance should end. The probability of it ending is no more or less than when the advance began. There are many examples of stocks that have experienced sustained price moves. Sometimes these moves cover hundreds of dollars.

The point is simple. You should be watching what the market is actually doing rather than stubbornly refusing to believe it is happening. I make it a policy not to get involved in these stocks because I have done no real research on them. Don't be tempted by the hysteria of the stock market. Many emotions will interfere with your investment decisions. We all know about fear and greed. But how many times have you actually become angry at the outcome of a trade. Getting angry at the market will not do you much good except to cloud your thinking.

Know thyself

Technical analysis attempts to provide us with the objective approach to the market which we seek. If you are simply doing what your charts tell you to then you won't get emotionally wrapped up in specific events. A chart may give a "buy" signal even after a stock has experienced a significant advance. The chart is incapable of saying "Eventually it must go down." For the record, I am not actually a great fan of technical analysis (for other reasons) but I admire what it attempts to accomplish. I also acknowledge that it is useful as an investment tool. The greatest shortcoming of using such a system exclusively is the temptation to predict in advance the patterns that the charts will take; and interpret them before the event has occurred. It is these types of interpretations that lead technicians down the road to destruction. Ironically, technicians suffer losses because they do not trust the tool that they swear by. They should simply listen to the chart rather than to themselves.

Before you invest, you should assess your needs, research the particular investment you are contemplating, and understand its potential risk and reward. In terms of its risk, you want to limit your exposure to an acceptable level. It is normally easy to do this with a stock since you can physically place a stop-loss order with your broker. Unfortunately, stop-loss orders are not available with options. Extra care must be taken to mentally establish some level at which you will take yourself out of a trade. This is especially true for uncovered options. The stop-loss order actually has an excellent application for winning trades. When a stock has experienced an advance, you can protect some of your profits by establishing a price at which you will exit. In the meantime, if the stock continues to advance you will continue to profit. It is a simple matter to change the stop-loss limit upward and continue to profit from the stock's advance. This will allow you to adhere to the advice of some of the most successful investment advisers: Keep your winners and sell your losers.

Many experiences await an option trader; indeed, I hope that some of the real-life anecdotes in this book will give the reader some idea of the variety I have had trading options. There is no substitute for experience, they say, and it is particularly true when it comes to the stock market. It is not enough to trade on paper to learn how to trade stocks or options. Knowledge is not all that is required to be successful. Without actually entering into a trade you will never know how you will react to winning and losing situations.

The Greek philosopher Socrates admonished his pupils to "Know thyself." This advice will serve you well in the stock market. One of my particular problems in the market was when to exit trades. But not losing trades. Those were easy, since I hate losing money. It was the winning trades that I was always getting wrong. I was too impatient and nervous when I had a winner. I would always exit the trade too early and miss out on a significant profit. Not an uncommon malady, but one that cannot be cured unless you are actually trading in the market.

Know your stocks

At a recent financial conference, a woman approached me and explained that she had been losing a lot of money trading options. She had a good understanding of options and how they were traded but continued to lose money. I assumed that she was going to tell me that she had been trading them for short-term gains and was attempting to time the market. Wrong. To my surprise, she had been buying and holding long-term, in-the-money calls. In other words, she was using options as I recommend using them.

What advice did I give her? Well, it was obvious that options were not the culprit in her case. It is a poor workman who blames his tools. But this does not also mean that just because you use options properly you cannot lose money. The fact is, she was simply not picking stocks very well. Luckily, because she was using long-dated options the losses were not as large as they might have been if she had been buying stocks. But her research was incomplete. The underlying stocks were simply not performing as she had hoped. Nothing to do with options really. The moral of this story is obvious: Do your research before making any investment. There is no replacement for investment knowledge and definitely no option strategy which will allow you to profit without making an educated decision on the underlying security.

Some final words

My intent has been to arm the reader with a basic knowledge of options and I hope that you have come away with some added knowledge of the marketplace and the role that options play. In closing, I will leave the reader with a gentle challenge. I especially recommend it for those who are cynical about the value of using options in their portfolio. The challenge is this: Review your last two years of stock trading. Calculate whether you would be ahead if you had simply purchased at-the-money calls instead of the stocks. In many cases, I think you will find that some of your losses would not have been as large, and some of your profits would have been better. And I think you will be surprised at the results.

Option Dynamics: The Greeks

I WOULD LIKE TO CONFESS that I was tempted to call this appendix, "It's all Greek to me." But that name has already been used for a seminar which is given by the Options Institute in Chicago. Owned and operated by the Chicago Board Options Exchange, the Options Institute is a non-profit organization and the leader in options education in the United States. They can be reached at 1-800-OPTIONS for information and questions regarding courses, literature or simply events in the marketplace.

This appendix defines some of the pricing concepts used by professional option traders. Bear in mind that most sophisticated traders have advanced computer programs to perform these calculations. Lesser mortals like you and me have to make do with electronic calculators to make these calculations. The performance of these concepts within your option strategy will for the most part be transparent. But I have included them to illustrate that the pricing of options is not some haphazard process. Market-makers do not "play dice with the universe." Many professional traders seek to execute option trades with the intention of completely avoiding the directional risk of the underlying stock. To do so, they implement hedging strategies and spreads utilizing the concepts listed below.

Beta

The beta is a measure of the relation between the movement of a particular stock and the market as a whole. Remember that the rate of change in the price of a stock is represented by a percentage figure stated as the volatility. Beta is not concerned with how fast this change takes place, just the amount of change. To see how the beta compares to the volatility of an underlying stock, you need only compare the actual volatility of the stock to the volatility of the market. The beta coefficient is expressed as a factor of 1. A stock with a volatility which is the same as the volatility of the market is said to have a volatility of 1. The beta is derived by dividing the volatility of the stock by the volatility of the market. Therefore, when the volatility of a stock is 20 per cent and the volatility of the market is 10 per cent, the stock will have a beta coefficient of 2. If the market advances by 10 per cent, a stock with a beta of 2 will advance by 20 per cent. Stocks with a beta of greater than 1 will move at a faster rate than the market and stocks with a beta of less than 1 will move at a slower pace. They will also decline at similarly proportionate rates during the event of a market decline. For this reason, high beta stocks can be regarded as somewhat riskier than stocks with a lower beta. Bear in mind that the particular stock must have some meaningful representation in the market. For instance, a stock which is heavily influenced by the price of gold will not merely respond to the movements of the market as a whole. For this reason, the beta is always an approximation. It is impossible to perfectly relate an individual stock to some event which influences the price of another stock in the index. Just because a takeover bid occurs on a particular stock, moving the index higher, does not necessarily mean that some other stock will move accordingly.

Systemic risk relates to the tendency of securities to move as a group or together. When you are vulnerable to the general price movement of the market you have systemic risk in your portfolio. You may own shares in a company that is also heavily weighted in an index, such as IBM in the Dow 30 industrial index. In the event of a market decline of the Dow 30, you may be surprised to see your shares decline along with the rest of the market. This may happen even though there is no news which seems to directly affect the fortunes of IBM. This is merely the result of investor sentiment in the market in general — the type of risk that cannot be immediately offset through the tactic of diversifying in other securities. In short, it is a risk which is not necessarily associated with the price movement of a specific security.

A gold stock may respond proportionately to a change in the price of gold as opposed to a general market move. This type of risk is specifically related to some underlying commodity and would be classified as non-systemic risk. So would some other event which had a direct event on the fortunes of a particular stock, such as a strike. To a degree, non-systemic risk can be countered by diversification. You could buy stocks in several industries or with different maturities. But this will not necessarily remove the risk of a market change on the whole.

Portfolio managers attempt to adjust their portfolios to eliminate risk by using an option which will replicate the movement of the market according to the expected rate of change in their underlying securities. To do this they use index futures and options in an amount proportionate to the beta of their portfolio. It is not enough to merely sell an amount of index options which covers the underlying value of their portfolio. For instance, if a portfolio were worth $100,000,000 with the index at 500, it would be a simple matter to sell 2,000 calls or buy 2,000 puts or a combination of both. But this could result in a loss if their portfolio did not move in exact proportion to the market. The beta of their portfolio will dictate how many calls or puts to buy or sell to hedge themselves against an adverse move in the underlying market. This will only be an approximation, because it cannot be known exactly what the relation of a stock to the overall market is because the many variables and conditions are constantly changing. No matter how many futures or options a portfolio manager sells, there will still be a small discrepancy between the value of the portfolio and the market after an adverse move. This discrepancy is also known as tracking error. If the discrepancy results in a profit, then it is known as a positive tracking error. A loss is known as a negative tracking error.

Buying a diversified portfolio of index stocks and selling the appropriate amount of futures or index options is basically what that evil thing known as program trading is all about. Index arbitrage, on the other hand, is the process of purchasing an exact amount of the underlying stocks composing the index and selling an exact amount of futures. If the futures are overpriced in relation to the stocks, then arbitrage traders will sell the futures and purchase the stocks. If stocks are overvalued or the futures are trading at a discount to the cash equivalent of the stocks in the index, then they will purchase the futures and sell the stocks. You can see that in a period where the market is moving quite rapidly, up or down, that this process can escalate the movement in the market. The speed of the advance or decline continues to create discrepancies between the price of the market compared with the futures/index contracts.

Gamma

Market-makers and portfolio managers sometimes attempt to avoid directional risk by maintaining delta neutral positions. Their biggest difficulty is that with the change in the underlying stock, the delta will also change. The delta is really only a measurement of the price an option is expected to move for the first point movement in the underlying stock. After some movement in the underlying stock, the delta of the option will actually change. If the stock advances by one point, then the delta of the at-the-money call may not remain at −0.50. When this happens, then the position becomes net long, or long deltas. Remember, the delta of the stock will always be 1, but the delta of the option as it goes further out-of-the-money will decline. The rate of change in the delta of an option is known as the gamma. The passage of time also affects the delta of an option. This is because as the option approaches expiry, its time value erodes to a point where parity is reached. An in-the-money option that started with a delta of 0.80 will eventually reach a point, close to expiry, where its delta is virtually 1. This is because the option can be exercised and a resulting stock position created. The stock position would have a delta of 1. If the delta were to remain at 0.80 then an easy profit could be realized by purchasing the option, exercising it and selling the stock. Think back to the discussion of intrinsic value. You were able to capture the intrinsic value of an option, regardless of its actual price, by simply purchasing it and exercising your option. In short, the gamma allows a professional to calculate how fast a position that may have been delta neutral can become long or short given the passage of time and movement of the underlying stock.

Theta

Theta is the rate of decline in the price of an option over its lifetime. It has no relation to the price of the underlying security. The decline in price referred to here deals only with the time decay of the option. It is best illustrated as the rate of decline in the price of an at-the-money option over the life of the option. In other words, it is the decline in the time value rather than the intrinsic value of the option. The rate of decay over time can be expressed as a price movement in relation to time only. And because it represents a decline in price, it is expressed as a negative number. If an option has a theta of .025, the option will lose 2.5 cents for each day that passes in the life of the option. Remember in the discussion concerning which option to purchase, I recommended a longer-term option to avoid the loss in value from the passage of time. Longer-term options will have a very low theta and near-term options will have a very high theta. From this you can see that the theta of an option will increase as the option approaches expiry. This is because the time decay of an option is not a straight-line phenomenon. The higher the premium of the option, the greater the potential time decay, or the greater the theta. Options with higher volatility will have a greater theta than low volatility options. They have more premium, and therefore a faster time decay.

Vega

Linguistic students may note that there is no actual letter of the alphabet known as vega. Others are also offended by this lexicographical misnomer and prefer to call it the "tau." By any other name, vega is still defined as the change in the value of an option that results in a change in the volatility in the underlying stock. You have seen that the price of an option will be correspondingly greater the higher the volatility becomes. Remember that volatility is one of the main components in the price of an option. It is also one of the most difficult to accurately quantify.

Recently, a colleague of mine purchased some May 40 call options on a stock that was trading at $38, for a price of $3 per option. The stock subsequently declined to $32. Sometime later the stock recovered to a level of $37. Oddly enough, the price of the call options actually rose to a level higher than his original purchase, even though the stock was still lower than at the time of the call purchase. Why? Even though some time had passed and the stock was now lower, the volatility had increased dramatically. This caused the premiums on the options to expand. His calls were now worth $3.25. There will come a time in your life when you purchase an option, see the underlying stock advance accordingly, only to see the price of the option actually decline. You have been the victim of a volatility decline. Option traders will often say that they are "long volatility" or "short volatility." They simply mean that they are net purchasers of options, because of their exposure to an increase or decline in the volatility of the underlying stock. This has absolutely no effect on the price of the underlying stock.

Then how can I calculate the effect of its change on the price of an option you may ask? Think back to the discussion on option pricing. Remember that you assigned the underlying stock an implied volatility figure for purposes of calculating the price of an option. Taking the leap that you have closely approximated the actual volatility of that stock, you can now process assumptions for the price of the option based upon what you view as possible changes to that volatility figure. Unlike the delta, the vega is always expressed as a positive figure. This is because you are always concerned with the net change in the price of the option in relation to the change in the volatility. If an option has a vega of 0.5 then a per cent increase in the implied volatility of the option will translate into a 50-cent increase in the price of that option. Similarly, a 1 per cent decline in the implied volatility will translate into a 50-cent decline in the price of the option. Oddly enough, vega is also related to time. The longer the life span of the option, the greater the vega will be, or the greater the effect a change in the implied volatility will be on its price. Vega will also be the highest for the options that will be most affected by a change in the implied volatility. This means that the at-the-money options will be most greatly affected. The vega can be calculated for a single stock option position or for an entire portfolio of options.

Rho
The rho is the measure of the change in the price of an option in relation to a change in the prevailing risk-free interest rate. Interest rates are one of the major factors in the pricing of an option. The higher the prevailing interest rate, the more it will cost an investor to carry a stock position. For a market-maker performing conversions it means that he will have to receive a larger premium from the sale of the call to pay for the cost to carry the stock. The effect of a rise in interest rates is to increase the price of calls and decrease the price of puts. Market-makers will also be willing to pay more for the purchase of a call option when rates are higher because it is part of the hedge or arbitrage equation in a reconversion. This is simply because when they sell the stock short they will be receiving a greater return on the proceeds of the short sale. At the same time, if they are receiving a better return on the short sale, then it will not be necessary to receive as much on the sale of the put. Thus, more puts will be sold and more calls will be bought, affecting the prices

accordingly. Calls will see their prices increase and puts will decrease.

Learning to speak Greek

With the exception of the delta, none of these factors can be used for the actual interest underlying an option. Stock has only delta. All of these concepts are basically just risk evaluations that a market-maker, or some other sophisticated investor, employs to analyze a particular position. The operative word in options pricing is theoretical. You cannot calculate the true value of an option with absolute certainty. It is merely a theoretical approximation. This, of course, is because you cannot know for certain the future volatility of the underlying stock. You can only assign it a volatility based upon its historical performance. These pricing concepts merely assist in defining characteristics of an option at a particular point in time. But they also illustrate how the position will change given certain changes in the marketplace. The average investor will rarely be making such exact and complex calculations when investing in options. But it is useful to see that the components that make up the price of an option, such as volatility, price movement and interest rates, are calculated by professionals to assess the risk and reward of a particular position. To see how arcane these calculations can actually become, there is something called the gamma of the gamma. The gamma of the gamma is a measure of the change in the gamma of a portfolio in relation to a change in price in the underlying stock. I mention it here only to make you aware of the depth to which you can take these mathematical calculations for the purpose of hedging and controlling risk.

A Glossary of Options Terms

AMERICAN-STYLE OPTIONS can be exercised at any time during their lifetime.

ARBITRAGE is the practice of buying and selling identical securities, simultaneously, for profit.

AS-YOU-LIKE-IT OPTIONS are not defined by type until a certain date, at the discretion of the buyer.

ASIAN OPTIONS have their settlement value determined by the difference between the exercise price and the average price of the underlying security during the life of the options.

ASSIGNMENT is the notification to the seller of an option that he has been called upon by the holder of that option to fulfill the terms of the contract. Notification is made by the clearing corporation.

AT-THE-MONEY OPTIONS have an exercise price that is the same as the price of the underlying security. Commonly used to describe any options whose exercise price is also very near to the price of the underlying interest.

AUTOMATIC EXERCISE happens when a clearing corporation exercises an option without receiving notice from the holder of the option.

BACK SPREAD is a spread comprised of more long options than short options. It is designed to profit from large swings in the underlying interest.

BASKET is a group of securities normally having some common characteristic, such as the components of a stock index.

BEAR SPREAD is a spread of equal numbers of puts or calls that seeks to profit from a decline in price of the underlying security.

BETA is the ratio of the movement of a particular stock or group of stocks in relation to the movement of the market as a whole.

BINARY OPTIONS have the writer pay a fixed amount once the underlying security reaches the exercise price. The amount is limited by the exercise price and it does not matter how high or low the underlying security rises or falls.

BLACK-SCHOLES MODEL is a mathematical model designed to calculate the theoretical value of an option.

BOX SPREAD is the simultaneous purchase of one call and sale of one put, or vice versa, at one exercise price and the purchase of one call and sale of one put at a second exercise price. It is a four-sided spread.

BULL SPREAD is a spread of equal numbers of puts or calls that seeks to profit from an advance in the price of the underlying security.

BUTTERFLY SPREAD is a spread involving the purchase of four calls or puts with three different exercise prices. It has limited risk and limited profit.

BUY-WRITE is the practice of simultaneously purchasing a stock and selling an equivalent number of calls.

CALENDAR SPREAD is a spread involving the purchase and sale of two calls or puts expiring in different months. This is also known as a horizontal spread.

CALL is a contract that grants the holder the right, but not the obligation, to purchase a specified amount of a defined security at an agreed-upon price for a stated period of time.

CARRYING COST is the amount of funds in terms of interest-rate charges that would be incurred to purchase a security.

CASH SETTLEMENT is a method of settlement of the exercise or assignment of certain options, such as index options, whereby an amount of cash is determined according to the difference between the exercise price and the level of the underlying security.

CHRISTMAS TREE SPREAD is an option spread involving six options and four exercise prices. One option is a lower strike, the second exercise price is skipped, three options are sold at the next strike, and two are purchased at the next strike. Similar to the butterfly, it has limited risk and limited profit.

CLASS is all options of the same type, calls or puts, having the same underlying security.

CLEARING CORPORATION is an organization that guarantees and settles all exchange-listed option transactions.

CLOSING TRANSACTION is a trade made to settle an existing option position. If the existing position was a purchase, the trade would be a corresponding sale, and vice versa.

COLLAR is neither a spread nor a combination. It is a position consisting of a short put and a long call with different strike prices. The strike price of the call is higher than the put.

COLLATERAL is security posted to guarantee the settlement of an anticipated option exercise.

COMBINATION is the purchase or sale of two puts or calls with different strike prices, having the same expiry month and the same underlying interest.

CONDOR SPREAD is a variation of the butterfly spread. One option is purchased at the lower strike price, one sold at the next strike, another option sold at the next strike, and one purchased at the higher strike.

CONTINGENCY ORDER is an order given to a floor trader to execute a trade only if certain conditions can be met. A buy-write is normally placed as a contingency order.

CONVERSION is the practice of purchasing a long call and selling a short put (synthetic stock), and simultaneously selling the corresponding stock for a locked-in profit.

COVERED STRADDLE is a strategy of purchasing a stock and selling a corresponding number of puts and calls, having the same strike price and expiry month.

COVERED STRANGLE is a strategy of purchasing a stock and selling a corresponding number of puts and calls, having the same expiry month but different strike prices.

COVERED WRITE is a strategy combining the purchase of a stock and the sale of a corresponding number of calls.

CREDIT SPREAD is the execution of a spread where the proceeds will be a credit to the investor. A bullish put price spread and a bearish call price spread are both normally credit spreads.

CYCLE is the number of months and the regularity in which options are listed on the exchange. For example, January-April-July-October is known as a January cycle.

DEBIT SPREAD is the execution of a spread where the result is a debit to the investor. A bullish call price spread and a bearish put price spread are normally debit spreads.

DEEP-IN-THE-MONEY describes an option that has a great deal of intrinsic value and, normally, very little or no time value.

DELTA is the anticipated amount of change in the price of an option for every one-point change in the price of the underlying security.

DELTA NEUTRAL is the practice of establishing a position that will not profit or loss from a directional move in the underlying security.

DIAGONAL SPREAD is a spread combining the purchase or sale of calls or puts having different strike prices and different expiry months.

DISCOUNT describes the price of an in-the-money option which has no time value and is trading for less than its intrinsic value in the market.

EARLY EXERCISE is the event of exercising a put or call prior to its expiry.

EUROPEAN-STYLE OPTIONS cannot be exercised by the holder prior to their expiry.

EXERCISE is the action of forcing the settlement of a put or call and imposing the terms of the contract by delivering a notice to the clearing corporation.

EXERCISE LIMIT refers to the number of options that may be tendered for exercise within a five-day period.

FENCE is a long call and a short put with different exercise prices having the same expiry month.

GAMMA is the amount of anticipated change in the delta on an option for a one-point change in the price of the underlying security.

HAIRCUT is the amount of margin required of a market-maker. It is called a haircut because it is somewhat less than the amount required for the public.

HEDGE is a combination of two or more securities designed to protect each other from a loss. For example, the sale of a futures contract can be hedged by purchasing an equivalent amount of the underlying security.

HISTORICAL VOLATILITY is a record of the actual price changes over a period of time for a given security.

HORIZONTAL SPREAD is a spread utilizing puts or calls of the same strike price, having different expiration months.

IMPLIED VOLATILITY is a percentage figure used in a pricing model to determine an option's price, or the amount that proves that price.

IN-THE-MONEY is the amount that the price of a security exceeds, in the case of a call, or is below, in the case of a put, the strike price of the option.

INDEX OPTION is an option whose underlying security is an index.

INDEX is a composition of an average of the prices of several securities. An index is normally weighted by price of the security or by the capitalization of the securities.

INTRINSIC VALUE is the amount, if any, which would result from the exercise of a put or a call after the resulting position in the underlying security was disposed of, or purchased, in the marketplace.

JELLY ROLL SPREAD is a combination of a long call and a short put in one expiry month, and a corresponding short call and long put in another expiry month.

LEG refers to one component of a position such as a spread. There are two legs to a covered write, the long stock and the short call.

LEGGING IN (OR OUT) is the practice of executing a position requiring two legs in a non-simultaneous fashion, such as purchasing the long stock in a covered write first and later selling a call.

LEVERAGE is the practice of controlling a greater amount of value of a security with a lesser amount of capital, such as borrowing the funds to purchase a stock.

LIMIT ORDER is an order that specifies a particular price for execution.

LOCAL is an independent floor trader with no affiliation to a particular company. He trades for personal profit on the floor of the exchange.

LOOK-BACK OPTIONS, at the end of their life, give the holder the choice of exercise at the highest level the underlying security reached.

MANUAL EXERCISE is the act of an individual tendering an exercise notice to a broker or clearing corporation.

MARGIN refers to the amount of capital required by the exchange for a particular securities transaction.

MARK-TO-MARKET is the practice of identifying the liquidation price of a given position at any particular time. Short stock positions are frequently marked-to-market to determine the amount of cash required to repurchase.

MARKET-MAKER is a trader on the floor of an exchange who has the responsibility of posting bids and offers in a particular security and is also employed by or is a member of, that exchange.

MARKET-MAKER SYSTEM ensures liquidity in a security by assigning it a market-maker.

MARRIED PUT is a strategy of purchasing a security and simultaneously purchasing a put option to protect its price. It is also known as a synthetic call.

MULTIPLIER is the amount that an option's price must be multiplied by to arrive at the dollar value of an option. The multiplier of an equity option is 100 because the contract covers 100 shares of stock. Index options are usually assigned a multiplier of 100.

NET ORDER is the net cost or proceeds of the execution of more than one position. A buy-write is normally executed at a net-debit to the investor, the cost of the stock minus the proceeds of the call.

NEUTRAL refers to the anticipation that a stock or the market as a whole will not move up or down.

NON-SYSTEMIC RISK is the risk incurred from exposure to a specific area of the market or economy. This risk is incurred when an investor is not diversified and has all of his funds invested in a particular security or industry group, such as gold stocks.

OPEN INTEREST is the number of contracts that have been purchased or sold not being offset by a closing transaction, on any given series of option.

OPTION WRITER describes the seller of an option where a corresponding long position is not held.

OUT-OF-THE-MONEY is the amount that the exercise price of an option exceeds in the case of a call, or is below in the case of a put, the price of the underlying security.

OVERVALUED refers to the notion that the price an option is trading at is above its theoretical value.

OVERWRITE is the practice of writing more calls or puts than are considered covered by another option or by the underlying security.

PARITY is a term used to describe the amount by which an option is in-the-money, or its intrinsic value. When an option is trading for exactly this amount it is said to be at parity.

PAY-LATER OPTIONS have their premiums paid by the purchaser at the end of the life of the contract.

PIN RISK is the risk in a conversion or reconversion position where the underlying stock is finishing exactly at-the-money and a market-maker is unsure of how many calls or puts are to be exercised.

POSITION LIMIT is the maximum number of option or future contracts that an individual is permitted to purchase or sell.

PREMIUM is the amount the option is trading at in the marketplace. This term is sometimes used to describe the amount of time value of an option.

PRICE SPREAD is the purchase or sale of calls or puts having the same expiry month and on the same underlying security but having different exercise prices.

PRIMARY MARKET is the market or exchange on which an option or stock is originally listed.

PUT OPTION is a contract granting the holder the right, but not the obligation, to sell a specific quantity of a security at a particular price for a stated period of time.

RAINBOW OPTIONS have several underlying securities. They are also known as basket options.

RECONVERSION is the practice of selling a call option and buying a put option (synthetic short stock) and simultaneously purchasing the underlying stock to lock in a profit.

REPAIR STRATEGY is a strategy designed to restore a losing stock or option position to a break-even point.

RHO is the anticipated change in the price of an option for a one-percentage-point change in current interest rates.

RISK ARBITRAGE is the practice of purchasing stock that is subject to a takeover bid in anticipation that the stock will in fact be taken over, but it assumes the risk that the stock will fall if the bid is withdrawn.

ROLLING is the practice of simultaneously closing out one option position and establishing a different option position on the same underlying security, thereby extending the term or adjusting the exercise price.

ROLLING DOWN is the practice of purchasing or selling an option and re-purchasing or re-selling an option on the same underlying security, but with a lower strike price.

ROLLING IN is the practice of purchasing or selling an option and repurchasing or reselling an option on the same underlying security, but with a nearer-term expiry month.

ROLLING OUT is the practice of purchasing or selling an option and repurchasing or reselling an option on the same underlying security but with a longer-term expiry month.

ROLLING UP is the practice of purchasing or selling an option and repurchasing or reselling an option on the same underlying security, but with a higher exercise price.

ROTATION is a method of opening an option class for trading. Each series is opened individually until the entire class has been rotated.

SANDWICH SPREAD is a version of the butterfly spread. The lower strike option is sold, the two middle strike options are purchased, and the higher strike option is purchased.

SECONDARY MARKET refers to the exchange where an option trades.

SERIES refers to each individual put or call on a given security.

SPREAD is a position composed of two or more securities which seeks to benefit from the difference between them, such as the price difference, time difference, etc.

STANDARD DEVIATION is a statistical calculation describing a change in price from within the normal distribution of prices of a given security.

STOP BUY ORDER is an order placed for execution requiring that a security be purchased at the best available price if it advances to a certain point.

STOP LIMIT ORDER is an order placed for execution requiring that the security be sold if it declines to a certain price, but specifying at the same time that it is not to be sold below a certain price.

STOP LOSS ORDER is an order placed for execution requiring that a security be sold at the best available price if it declines to a given price.

STRADDLE is the simultaneous purchase or sale of a call and a put on the same underlying security with the same exercise price and having the same expiry month.

STRAP is a strategy involving the purchase or sale of two calls and one put.

STRIP is a strategy involving the purchase or sale of two puts and one call.

SURROGATE STOCK describes a very deep-in-the-money call option.

SYNTHETIC OPTION is a term used to describe an alternative position with equal profit/loss potential. Long stock plus a long put is known as a synthetic call option.

SYSTEMIC RISK is the risk an investor assumes with an investment that the market as a whole, and not just a particular sector, may decline.

THEORETICAL VALUE is the calculated value of a security as opposed to the actual price it trades for in the market.

THETA is the anticipated amount of decline in the price of an option for the passing of one day in the life of that option. The theta is a calculation of the rate of that change.

TIME DECAY refers to the notion that an option loses some of its value over time. The measure of this rate of decline is known as the theta.

TIME VALUE is the difference between the exercise price of an option and its intrinsic value, if any.

TYPE, a listed option is one of two types, a put or a call.

UNDERLYING INTEREST is the security that can be bought or sold according to the terms of the option contract.

VEGA is the anticipation of the amount of change in the price of an option for a one-percentage-point change in the assumption of the volatility of the security.

WASTING ASSET is a security that loses its value over the course of time, assuming that there is no change in the value of the corresponding underlying interest. Options, warrants and rights are known as wasting assets.

WRITE means to sell, and thereby create, an option.

Bibliography

Confessions of an Options Strategist: A Winner's Guide to Profitable Option Trading, by Alexander M. Gluskin. Publisher: Hounslow (1990). Difficult to find, but worth it if you do. Gluskin emphasizes discipline and money management.

LEAPS: What They Are and How to Use Them for Profit and Protection, by Harrison Roth. Publisher: Irwin, Professional Publishing. Roth is a well known lecturer and writer in the U.S. He is also the option strategist at Cowen and Co. in New York. In his highly readable and enlivened style, he presents LEAPS in an easy to understand manner for the average investor.

Options as a Strategic Investment, by Lawrence G. McMillan. Publisher: New York Institute of Finance (1993). The Bible of option trading, but not inexpensive. A vast resource with in depth technical information on all aspects of options products and trading.

Options: Essential Concepts and Trading Strategies. Publisher: Business One Irwin Homewood. Written by several instructors at the Options Institute (CBOE). Many discussions of market making as well as institutional trading strategies.

Index

THE GLOBE AND MAIL PERSONAL FINANCE LIBRARY

The Globe and Mail Personal Finance Library is designed to help you build your wealth and achieve your goals. Just a few minutes a day reading our books will give you you the insights you need to manage your money more effectively. To complete your personal finance library use this convenient order form.

Mail to: **The Globe and Mail Personal Finance Library, 444 Front Street West, Toronto, Ontario M5V 2S9**

Call: **1 800 268-9128**
in Toronto: **416 585-5250**

Fax: **416 585-5249**

Visit: **Any bookstore that sells Penguin Books**

YES! *Please rush my order:*

(Indicate your selection at right)

☐ 10 books in The Globe and Mail Personal Finance Library for just **$99.99*** (a 33% saving)

☐ 8 books for just **$79.99*** (a 33% saving)

☐ 5 books for just **$49.99*** (a 33% saving)

☐ 3 books for just **$33.99*** (a 25% saving)

☐ Individual books are **$14.99***

☐ *The Only Retirement Guide You'll Ever Need* individual price **$19.99***

_____ Understanding Mutual Funds
_____ RRSPs 1996
_____ Investment Strategies
_____ The Money Companion
_____ Retire Right
_____ The Gold Book
_____ Bulls and Bears
_____ Money For Rent
_____ Insure Sensibly
_____ Exploring Options
_____ The Only Retirement Guide

Cost of books ordered	$ _____
* plus shipping & handling	$ 4.00
* plus 7% GST	$ _____
TOTAL	$ _____

Name _____

Address _____

City _____ Province _____ Postal Code _____

Daytime phone (include area code) (_____) _____

Payment by ☐ MC ☐ VISA ☐ AmEx ☐ Cheque enclosed

Account Number |_|_|_|_|_|_|_|_|_|_|_|_|_|_|_|_| Expiry date (m/y) |_|_| |_|_|

Signature _____